THIS IS WHERE I CAME IN

THIS IS WHERE
I CAME IN

Brian Matthew

Constable · London

First published in Great Britain 1991
by Constable and Company Limited
3 The Lanchesters, 162 Fulham Palace Road
London W6 9ER
Copyright © Brian Matthew 1991
The right of Brian Matthew to be
identified as the author of this work
has been asserted by him in accordance
with the Copyright, Designs and Patents Act 1988
ISBN 0 09 470290 x
Set in Monophoto 12pt Ehrhardt by
Servis Filmsetting Limited, Manchester
Printed in Great Britain by
St Edmundsbury Press Limited
Bury St Edmunds, Suffolk

A CIP catalogue record for this book
is available from the British Library

'The King's Breakfast' on p. 20 is reproduced from
When We Were Very Young by A.A. Milne
by permission of Methuen Children's Books.

ILLUSTRATIONS

A rare moment of quiet before the pandemonium of 'Lucky Stars'
Presenting Kenny Ball with a gold disc for 'Midnight in Moscow'
With Bobby Vee and his group, the V Men
A real band of DJs

INTRODUCTION

I belong to a generation that spent much of its formative years in a black and white world. At least once a week, and often two or three times, we spent hours in the comfortable darkness and strangely perfumed atmosphere of a local cinema. From bug-hutch to rococo palace, these bore the grandiose names of Ritz, Savoy, Gaumont and Empire: Rivoli, Tivoli, Plaza and Forum. But one thing they had in common and that was the proudly announced 'Continuous Performance'. There was always the main feature, known in my birthplace and no doubt in many another's as the Big Picture, and there was also the supporting film. Sandwiched between the two would be a Pathé or Gaumont British newsreel, maybe a cartoon or two, and trailers for the following week's attractions. There was often much swishing to and fro of velvet curtains followed by several layers of gossamer flimsies, usually illuminated in green or pink by overhead spotlights. The censor's certificate was always projected in rippling outline, quite illegible until the last of these Salome-like veils had been drawn aside.

But, unless you were in one of the grandest of cinemas – they sported a mighty Wurlitzer which rose majestically from a Stygian pit in front of the screen and was operated by a white-coated, smiling musician – the great thing was that once the day's programme had begun it went on remorselessly till closing time. This meant that most of us never bothered to check starting times because we were unlikely to miss anything anyway. We all seemed to acquire the knack of memorising instantly, once sitting comfortably, the location, dramatic situation or line of dialogue that was being screened at that particular moment. Then, when the

[7]

whole programme had rolled its way round to the same point, one of us would marshal a retreat with the stage whispered incantation, 'This is where we came in.'

Mind you, there was always someone who spoiled the symmetry of this sequence by adding, 'Let's see it round again!'

[I]

The year was 1951. Although there was still rationing and austerity in the wake of World War Two it had been decided that the second half of the twentieth century should be marked by a great Festival of Britain. The Queen herself laid one of the many foundation stones for a National Theatre, years before if not yards from the eventual appearance of that building.

A great theatrical occasion that had taken place a few months earlier, however, had been the re-opening of the Old Vic, restored after bomb damage during the war. An elderly but revered Dame Edith Evans prefaced the historic event with an afterwards much impersonated performance of a specially commissioned ode, 'London rejoice! Your Shakespeare's home again.' And there followed a wondrous performance of *Twelfth Night* with Peggy Ashcroft as Viola and Roger Livesey as Sir Toby Belch. Also in the cast as a walk-on was a girl who less than a year later was to become, and still is, my wife. At that stage we were unaware of each other's existence.

Indeed, while all these celebrations were going on in the Waterloo Road, I was still a student at the Royal Academy of Dramatic Art, the fortunate recipient of a grant from a grateful government in return for two years of my life serving King and Country as a conscripted soldier. (In truth, I had had a whale of a time playing at being a broadcaster in Hamburg, but more of that anon.)

How difficult it is now to recall, through the cloak of cynicism in which the passing years all too readily wrap us, the pure delight, idealism and euphoria of one's early twenties. Yet I do still have some inkling of my excitement when I was told, after the school show in my final term at RADA, that Hugh Hunt, director of the Old Vic, had been out front and had chosen six of us to join his company. This was the hand of destiny, surely, and fame and fortune could not be long delayed. I even had the audacity to turn down his original offer of four pounds ten shillings a week and felt for the first time the frisson of power on hearing the figure upped to five whole pounds!

It was a long time before I learned why the magnificent six had been plucked from obscurity. We were in fact insignificant pawns in a contest between the theatre and the actors' union, Equity. At this time there was still an Old Vic Theatre School, run by the directors, Michel St Denis, Glen Byam Shaw and George Devine, and in 1950 they had decided as an economy (and as a good idea anyway) to take a group of senior students on little or no pay into the company as extras and understudies. It is only fair to point out that at this time it was standard practice for repertory companies all over the country to employ 'students' as unpaid acting stage managers and general dogsbodies; there is no doubt that in many cases this was reprehensible exploitation. I don't believe this was the case with the Old Vic students, who were given the invaluable opportunity of practical experience alongside some of the cream of the profession. However, Equity was obviously concerned about what they saw as a dangerous precedent that might deny employment to humbler members of the business. So a formula was worked out whereby the Vic students could stay if the company agreed to audition and employ at minimum salaries students from another drama school.

The first new production in Festival Year was to be *Henry V*, directed by Glen Byam Shaw, with the golden voiced Alec Clunes in the title role. And what a cast had been assembled! Many of them, alas, no longer with us: Roger Livesey, who played the Chorus; William Devlin was Fluellen; and Rupert Davies – later a famous television Maigret – was Williams. Younger members of the company destined to become leading actors themselves included Dorothy Tutin, who played Katherine, and Richard Pascoe. The Constable of France was played by John Ebdon, more recently concerned with stars of a different kind as director of the London Planetarium. That fine actor Paul Rogers performed an impressive double as the Dauphin and the Duke of Burgundy; I had the honour of understudying him in both roles as well as playing the small part of the soldier Bates.

The sets and costumes had been designed by Motley, and the curtain went up on a stage bare but for six huge poles. Then, as we marched on, we pulled cords and down cascaded marvellous banners. The cynicism of the years has done nothing to mar that memory. Fresh from drama school, walking on at the Vic to open an exciting new production was my first time ever on a professional stage. Even as I write these words I can still feel the sensation, almost like vertigo, as though my legs would never carry me on and downstage.

Fortunately for the paying public I never did have to go on for my principal, though it came close at one point. Paul Rogers was not at all well for a short period and at one performance, between appearances, was lying in a cart in the wings. I made the mistake of asking him how he felt, which not surprisingly stirred him to growl, 'You bugger, you can't wait to go rushing on, can you!'

Then there was the awful, unspeakable occasion when I didn't go on, even in my own role. Well into the run, when much of a performance becomes automatic, a group of English soldiers had got things nicely timed to allow a visit to the below stage canteen for a cup of tea just before a battle sequence during which the French army was to be vanquished. Alas, the day came when we timed it less than well, and at the appropriate moment poor old Rupert Davies was the only member of the English side in the wings. He rushed on valiantly; the astonished French army had to feign fear and horror at this one-man attack and fled shrieking into the wings.

Rupert had, by this time, become my landlord in a manner of speaking. Knowing that I was in need of accommodation, he told me that he and his wife had had a most extraordinary piece of good luck. They had followed up an advertisement offering a free flat in Gloucester Terrace in return for modest duties as a janitor. He thought there was one room vacant which he could fix for me at a rent of three pounds a week. It was quite a while before we both discovered that we were the respectable front for the fact that all other tenants in the house were ladies of the night. It was quite a switch from the conventional view of actors as the rogues and vagabonds.

During the run of *Henry V* I met and fell in love with one of the Old Vic students, Pamela Wickington, and we became engaged. . . . Now it just so happens that most of the other young actors who had come with me from RADA to join the company left no doubt about their own sexual inclinations: they were outrageously camp. This prompted Alec Clunes to remark, on hearing of my engagement, that he was glad to see one of the more doubtful boys back on the right lines.

I like to think that today I should laugh at such a comment, but at the age of twenty-two I was furious and had the temerity to confront Alec in the canteen. When he knew what had upset me he very graciously apologised, but the reaction of other company members was quite different. One of them said I was a silly fool, because there I was with an opportunity handed me on a plate: 'I've been trying to convince Binkie I was that way for years!' Binkie Beaumont was one of the most powerful men in the theatre of that period, casting director for the mighty Tennant organisation, and the subject of much gossip about his alleged sexual preferences.

When *Henry V* came to the end of its initial run, the company was divided into two. One group went on an English tour with a double bill of *The Wedding* by Chekhov, and *Electra*, while the other took Shaw's play *Captain Brassbound's Conversion* on a British Council tour of Holland and Belgium.

One rainy afternoon in The Hague, almost the entire company was hotel-bound; most of us had no money and it was far too unpleasant for sight-seeing. By way of passing the time, one actor, Teddy Leslie, admitted that he dabbled a little in palm reading and offered to amuse us by telling our fortunes. Teddy was a tall, thin figure, with a quiet sense of humour and hooded lids over deep brown eyes. He was well liked among the younger set, but it was not at all difficult to believe that he might be clairvoyant. At all events, he seemed to take the matter seriously and certainly did not take the easy option of ambiguous predictions. When it came to my turn, he said, 'You are going to leave the theatre quite soon.' 'Rubbish,' I responded, rather crossly. 'I'm never going to quit the theatre. This is it, for life.' 'Nevertheless,' continued Teddy, 'it's quite plain in your palm that you are going to give it up, soon. You will then do something rather different, though in some ways still connected with entertainment, and you'll enjoy considerable success. Then much later in life you will come back to the theatre, and will have success as an actor.'

Despite the interval of almost forty years, I swear that is an almost verbatim account of our conversation that rainy afternoon in the Hague. And the disquieting thing about it is that, just over a year later, I had left the theatre and started on a career that was to prove both absorbing and rewarding. Even more amazing to me is that now, in my early sixties, that career is behind me, not by my own choice, and I have indeed gone back to the theatre.

But before going forward with my story, this seems to be the moment to go right back to the beginning.

[2]

I was born at 49 Westwood Road, Coventry, in a small terraced house backing on to a railway embankment, on September 17, 1928. It was a forceps delivery which left me with an indentation at the corner of my left eye that I have to this day, and a pointed head that I haven't.

There is no reason to suppose that my arrival had not been eagerly awaited, but my uncomely appearance certainly led to the following oft repeated dialogue:

'What a funny little thing,' from my father, followed by 'Oh, Joe!' and floods of tears from my mother.

Apart from my parents, the household consisted of my father's mother, already over seventy years old at my birth and destined to live with us for the next nineteen years; there was also a small mongrel named Spot that I don't remember at all. In fact, recollections of that first home are few, but two are graphic. I had a number of dolls of which the best-loved was a china-headed beauty known as Dolly Daydream, and my father set out to entertain me by using these dolls in his own interpretation of a Punch and Judy show. When Dolly Daydream, in the role of Punch's baby, was whacked on the kitchen table her china head was shattered to smithereens, reducing me to inconsolable grief.

The other memory is of being taken out for a walk by my Gran. Clad in a light-coloured hat, coat and gaiters buttoned down the sides, I plodded off to the corner of our road where there was a wet fish shop, whose wares were displayed on a trestle table outside the shop window. Beneath this table was a drain, I suppose about a foot deep, fed by a pipe from the shop. The temptation to crawl under the table and then to stand in this drain, incomprehensible as it is now, was then irresistible. Unfortunately the drain was narrow, even for a two year old, and once in I stuck firmly. Cries for help eventually persuaded my septuagenarian but devoted Gran to crawl in after me and haul me out, smelling to high heaven.

Presumably the place of my birth had been a rented house, for in 1932 we moved to a newly built one in Billing Road which was then on the extreme outskirts of the city, bordered by farmland, and, as it turned out, my mother and father's only venture into property ownership. There is a flickering image of that removal, too, for while my parents presumably accompanied the van with our home in it, Gran and I made the journey separately; I rode a tiny tricycle. Even today I find that mildly astonishing, for although many things that seem vast in childhood dwindle with the passing years, that journey still strikes me as a damned long way for three and a half year old legs to pedal.

But what a paradise that new little house turned out to be for a small boy. Not only did the back garden gate open on to fields for as far as one cared to walk, but through those fields meandered a brook which gave scope for paddling, dam-building, raft-making and fishing for sticklebacks: in summer a gentle stream but sometimes in winter a dangerously deep and swift-moving torrent. Not the least of its attractions was that on emerging from the fields it ran in a gully at the roadside for a while before disappearing into a tunnel under that road to appear again who knew where. It was many a day before we had the courage to explore the tunnel with torches, eventually stepping out into daylight again, gratefully, between allotments. This 'brook' is in fact the river Sherbourne and finds its way to the very centre of Coventry before disappearing again underground; in due course it joins the river Avon.

Billing Road is a short but fairly steep hill and at the top of it there was access between two houses to another wonderland called Hearsal Common. This was a labyrinth of pathways among gorse bushes leading to a clearing which lent itself to fairly rough forms of cricket. A little further away was a recreation area, with swings and roundabouts, constructed alongside a stone structure that had originally been a sheepfold. Built of large blocks it stood I suppose some six feet high and was easily scalable; a wide parapet ran round three sides, while in the front there were 'windows' containing iron spikes, and an opening with a gate long gone. What games we played there I now have no idea, yet when I took my wife to see it some years ago I felt a strange surge of grief to find it no longer existed. Could this have stemmed from some primordial instinct? For it was much later that I discovered one of my forebears had quite literally worked on that common for a crust.

When my mother died in 1986, we found among her possessions an old exercise book hand-written in pencil by her maternal grandfather, Thomas Leather, a watchmaker. The first two pages give a clear picture of what life was like for some relatively poor people a hundred and more years ago. I am proud to say that this man taught himself to read and write, and I quote him verbatim:

I can remember when I was at the age of four. I was the oldest son of John Leather, watchmaker. I was born at Prescott in Lancashire. My father being very short of work at that time, had to leave Prescott to look for work. He had to walk all the way from Prescott to Coventry where he found work. It was some considerable time before he found work in Coventry but after a time he succeeded and he thought it wise to send for his wife and family. I well remember the 4th November 1858, a bitter cold morning it was, and there was great distress for those whom we had been brought up with as children and neighbours and uncles and aunts had to leave the country (sic) into one we did not know. We had to ride both mother and children in a donkey cart all the way from Prescott to Liverpool as there was no station in between at that time.

When we arrived at Coventry station there was no one there to meet us excepting a good old man (who has now gone to rest) who took us to Earlsdon and there we stayed till my father could get a house for us. My father succeeded in getting a house, and it was very hard lines with us at that time, for work fell off and my father had to work upon the common for sixpence and a loaf per day which had to support my mother, myself and the children. We were only young then what could be done? My mother had to work from six o'clock in the morning till nine o'clock at night at washing in order that she might get bread for the children.

Whatever kind of work was poor old John doing on the common for sixpence a day, one wonders. Shepherding, perhaps? 'He was a man who liked drink, I am sorry to say,' my great grandfather records, and he seems to have been out of work as often as in.

At the age of nine young Thomas found work himself, turning a loom for three shillings and sixpence a week, which he stuck at, under-nourished as he was, for two or three years before his father apprenticed him to the watch trade. For the next ten years, Tom worked from eight in the morning till seven at night, bringing his tools home then to do more work from eight until nearly one in the morning, rising again at five to work until twenty to eight when he ate a frugal breakfast and then returned to his place of employment. Not surprisingly, this regimen resulted in a breakdown and the doctors held out little hope for his recovery. Nevertheless, he did recover and went back to work once more where, to use his own words again, 'I then had a task set for me I was to earn so much for my employer every week and drew my over money at the end of the quarter.'

Unfortunately from the historical point of view Thomas Leather was soon to be 'saved' by the Salvation Army and the rest of his journal turns into a fairly monotonous catalogue of sinners and redemption. We learn that he married, but are left wondering what kind of marriage this must have been, for he records neither his wife's name nor the fact that she bore him three children. He did have the grace to write, 'I must say that I married a good wife so far as goodness goes,' but seems to have been irritated by the fact that she had not herself been saved. She did at last see the light, but she still didn't get a name check. I recently discovered an entry in a tiny

[17]

Scripture Text Book with the information that she was Fanny
Leather and died in 1913 at the age of fifty-nine. I think I should
have liked my great-grandmother very much indeed, but I don't
think I'd have gone a bundle on sanctimonious Tom.

The other side of my family is something of a mystery. My Gran
was born to John Matthews (I don't know when that 's'
disappeared), cotton weaver, and his wife Jane Parkes on April 3,
1856 at 126 Tame Street, Manchester. She went into domestic
service and at the age of thirty-one was made pregnant by the
master of the house whose name I have never known: the secret
died with my mother. There is in the family album an unidentified
Manchester studio photograph of a man bearing a striking
resemblance to my father at about the same age and indeed not
unlike myself, but whether or not it is my grandfather I shall never
know. I believe an offer was made to adopt my father, but Gran
refused and instead was given a sum of money with which she set
herself up with a small bakery, supporting herself and Joseph
Samuel who was born on September 8, 1888 at Bent Lanes,
Davyhulme, Manchester. The boy had very little schooling,
leaving entirely at the age of eight to help in the bakery and on the
delivery round with the one employee.

Given that background I find it little short of astonishing that by
the time I made my father's acquaintance he had not only learned to
read and write music and to play every instrument in the brass
family, but had also studied harmony and counterpoint, and
arranged music for bands and for choirs. On top of that he
constantly read all the works of Dickens and Shakespeare, and had a
profound knowledge of both. There never seems to have been
thought of using these talents in a professional way, for young Joe's
music was learned and practised under the auspices of the Salvation
Army which was his only means of gaining access to instruments.
At some stage it would appear that the bakery was sold and my
father started to work in factories. Then, as had coincidentally been
the case with my maternal great-grandfather half a century earlier,
an economic recession in the north made my father look to the

burgeoning industrial city of Coventry. The once flourishing watch trade had diminished, and such as it was was conducted in small workshops built over the wash-houses of terraced houses, some of which are still there to this day, probably converted to bedrooms. The growing work force, which was also starting to include refugees from the Welsh coal mines, had turned first to the manufacture of bicycles and then to the rapidly expanding automobile industry.

I know that Dad served an apprenticeship as a mechanic with the firm of Alfred Herberts, but he seems to have worked for another firm where he fell foul of the Amalgamated Engineering Union. I never heard about this but have in my possession a letter from the General Secretary of the Union dated November 1922 about an appeal by 'Bro. J. Matthew', which the Executive Council had decided to uphold because they had not been aware that 'this member was employed at a non-Federated Firm'. However, he then went on to work for the famous Armstrong-Siddeley company and finally for Morris Motors, where he stayed until he retired; indeed my own first two cars were bought at the employees' discount through a man who had never been able to afford one for himself.

Joe also married at some stage, but by all accounts it was never a happy relationship. The lady became an invalid and died when my father was in his late thirties. Long before that he had met my mother through music. She was a contralto of some distinction and when only a teenager sang on occasions with the City of Coventry band for which my father was the principal euphonium player and eventually the conductor. Their friendship must have flourished, but I don't think my father was the kind of man who could ever have contemplated divorce, with the result that my mother was twenty-six years old by the time he was free to marry her in 1927.

There is a terrible irony in that here were two people, both talented musicians, yet both fated to spend their working lives in factories. And here am I, a musical duffer despite every opportunity and encouragement under the sun, and I have spent most of my working life associated with music and musicians.

The first school I attended was a fairly large one known as Centaur Road, and I fell in love with my first teacher, Miss Insley, who was very glamorous. She was guilty of two things which my mother believed to be immoral in those days. She used both nail varnish and lipstick!

What memories abide to this day; I recall Miss Insley reading to her class of five year olds A.A. Milne's poem 'The King's Breakfast':

> The King asked
> The Queen, and
> The Queen asked
> The Dairymaid:
> 'Could we have some butter for
> The Royal slice of bread?'

and so on. She then cast the piece for some of us to enact before the others. I was given the part of the King, and thoroughly enjoyed the early bits about 'sliding down the banisters', but disaster lay in store for me: towards the end of the poem there occurs the line 'The King kissed the Queen' and I couldn't for the life of me bring myself to do it, despite the willingness of the Queen and the cajoling, followed by orders, from my adored Miss Insley. I just didn't fancy my co-star, Brenda Fletcher. Poor Brenda. I'm sure she was a very nice girl and she certainly had a sense of humour: one day in another class, the teacher, emphasising her regret over something that had occurred, said, 'Oh, what a pity. Oh, a thousand pities,' and Brenda whispered, 'Pity, pity, pity, pity . . .' until asked what she was saying: 'Nothing, miss.' The Fletchers came to live almost opposite our house eventually and Brenda was always referred to by my mum as Pity Pity Fletcher.

My recollection of junior school is slight, but some things stand out, for instance the time I was first caned. Goodness knows what heinous offence I had committed, possibly talking in class. It stays in my mind not for the pain of the punishment but for the shame of it, and because I really liked the teacher who meted it out. His name was Mr Sharkey. He smoked a great deal and had a small toothbrush moustache, heavily stained by nicotine. But he also taught us way beyond the requirements of our age group for those days, introducing rudimentary chemistry and physics into the curriculum together with fascinating experiments. He undoubtedly gave a flying start to those of us lucky enough later to go to grammar schools.

There was one other teacher I recall, Mr Mann. He was a northerner with flat vowel sounds and a droning, boring voice. He was much more free with the cane than most of the others and he also had the kind of violent temper that strikes terror into the hearts of little boys. There seems to me now to have been something rather Dickensian about the fact that this unpleasant man taught religious instruction. 'I always tell boys', he used to say at least once a week, 'that the most excitin' 'istory book in the world is the Old Testament.' But I don't think he made many converts.

One more almost dreamlike recollection of that part of my life: in 1935 the whole school was taken to London for the Silver Jubilee celebrations of King George V and Queen Mary. We travelled from Coventry by train and went to Windsor, where we were given packed meals in cardboard boxes; it was in those boxes that I saw earwigs for the first time in my life. There followed a trip down the Thames on paddle steamers and so back home by train, clutching souvenir mugs.

It must also have been around this time that I had my first taste of live theatre for Dad took me on one occasion back-stage at the old Coventry Hippodrome. It had a stone facade rather like a castle, presumably to complement one of the old city gates which stood nearby. In that mysterious world beyond the stage door I saw people with strange clothes and painted faces; one in particular was dressed and made up as Charlie Chaplin. We were going by appointment to meet the conductor of the Hippodrome orchestra, Charles Shadwell, later to become famous as the director of the

BBC Variety Orchestra, and indeed someone I was destined to meet myself in my own early career at the BBC. But what the reason might have been for that first encounter I never knew, unless my father was trying to obtain part-time work as a copyist. If so he must have been unsuccessful, for we never went there again.

I was taken, though, to the Shakespeare Memorial Theatre, as it was then called, in Stratford-on-Avon to see a performance of *Hamlet*. I was eight years old and I think I slept through a great deal of the play, but I did see the great Donald Wolfit, who had played the Prince, hang on the curtain at the end exactly as Albert Finney would, playing the part of Wolfit, years later in Ronald Harwood's play *The Dresser*; I heard him deliver his regular curtain speech which always began, 'From the depth of my being, I thank you....'

That theatre party must have been organised by either the choir or the dramatic society of Queen's Road Baptist Chapel, which was central to my parents' lives for many many years. Sundays for all of us meant morning service at eleven, followed by Sunday school in the afternoon, and then chapel service again in the evening, often followed by a social hour in the large hall where, after tea and biscuits, people sang and played instruments or performed monologues. It was this social hour that led to the first dramatic appearance of my own that I can remember. My mother had been booked to sing on one occasion, and on the preceding Saturday evening she was taken ill. Now two of my favourite books at that time were collections of monologues, and I had read and re-read them many times. The characters were all stereotypes: the Frenchman, the Doctor, the Parson and so on, and the one that appealed to me most was the Village Idiot. I said that if Mum liked I would take her place and recite this piece. She and Dad doubted that I could ever learn it in time, not realising that I already knew it backwards. I don't remember much of it now, which is probably just as well in view of the terrible jokes it contained, but a bit of it went something like this:

Oi be Billy. They calls oi silly Billy, but oi bain't so daft as oi looks. Oi saw Farmer Brown t'other day and I sez to 'im, oi've just seen your prize pork on the road. Why, don't 'ee be so silly, Billy, 'e sez to oi, pigs bain't pork till they're dead. Oi knows that. I sez, and yours be pork all roight, a motor car's just run over it.

It was appalling, but given the circumstances it went like a bomb. For the first time I experienced the intoxication of laughter followed by tumultuous applause. There was even fan mail: one letter I think drawing a parallel with the little Dutch boy who saved the day by putting his finger in a leaking dyke, which I must admit was a bit over the top.

Some time later, a whole show was put together from several Nonconformist churches, and we toured the city for a week or more. I was always chaperoned, of course, which was probably just as well because I developed an unrequited passion for the chubby half of an accordion duo, but never found out her name. I liked these evenings best when I was escorted by my beloved Aunty Mim, who had been my mum's best friend when they both worked in a factory during World War One. Mim, whose real name was Miriam, was not married herself at that time; she was a wonderfully jolly person, with a considerable gift for mimicry that enhanced her story telling. She also had the skill to perform quite simple conjuring tricks; a marble placed in the top of a candle-stick would disappear, only to re-appear in the top of another one, for instance. It was pure magic to me. When she brought me home from my 'Silly Billy' performances we always stopped at a fish and chip shop in Spon Street where I first developed a love of cod's roe!

My best friend until our ways parted at the age of ten or eleven was an elfin faced little chap named John Johnson, the son of a butcher. His parents were an oddly assorted couple indeed: Mrs Johnson a tiny, physically frail though I suspect spiritually strong woman, a former nurse and almost completely deaf, and Mr Johnson a big bodied, florid faced man, fond of his beer and very loud of voice. His favourite word was 'bloody' which I suppose was apposite in view of his trade and it occurred to me later that his normal manner of address, to shout everything, was because of his wife's handicap.

Mr Johnson worked for a master butcher in the heart of the old city and he did most of the work, which he was all too ready to demonstrate to John and me. He had, I remember, a succession of Austin Seven soft top cars and the one I liked best was a bright canary yellow. Whilst driving he would frequently leave one beefy arm hanging out of the window and beat his hand against the door whilst roaring some invocation to the car such as, 'Come on me old beauty, get a bloody move on!'

During school holidays, on Thursday afternoons, it was a special treat for John and myself to be taken to the neighbouring country market town of Hampton-in-Arden for the poultry and livestock auctions. We were allowed to wander unattended through the various buildings, hanging over pens containing sheep and standing amongst the crowd of farmers and butchers while cattle were paraded round the auction ring. At the end of the afternoon we usually had to share the back of the Austin with crates of squawking, defecating and rather smelly chickens. Then came the gruesome part of the day. In a small outbuilding behind the butcher's shop, Johnson senior took each chicken in turn, tied its legs together, suspended it from a hook in the ceiling and pierced its neck with a penknife. While the blood poured on to the stone floor he then set about plucking the carcase. It was a horrid sight, but nothing compared with one occasion on which the dead and plucked bird, still suspended from the hook, opened its eyes and raised its head to let out a last squawk.

Why this story of slaughter should put me in mind of one about salvation, I am not sure but indeed it does. On one occasion the infant river Sherbourne near our house became a flooded and fast-moving torrent, swirling through the duct that led to one of its underground sections. A boy whose name is long since obliterated from my memory foolishly pushed young John into the flood and then ran away. By climbing over the parapet and hanging down I managed to catch John's hand; eventually I hauled him out and

[24]

escorted him home, dripping and squelching every inch of the way.

Summer holidays at this period of my life were always spent in the then sleepy little South Devon resort of Dawlish, which bore little resemblance to the urban sprawl now connecting it almost continuously with Teignmouth to the south, and extending inland to the west up on to Haldon moor. From the age of ten months I was taken every year, first for one week and later for two, to stay in a cottage with the Wilson family who spoke the broadest Devonshire dialect you could hear. The father, Frank, had been a navy man in World War One, but I remember him first as the skipper of an open motor boat running trips in the bay and along the coast, then as a deckchair man on Dawlish beach, as the local postman, and finally as a ticket collector at the station. In late life he decided to learn to play the accordion and against all odds made quite remarkable progress, helped by long nightly tuition from my father.

Frank's wife Annie addressed all and sundry, in true Devonshire fashion, as 'my dear' and had a wonderful sense of humour. She long outlived her husband and many years on I was able to visit her, to her great delight, with my own little boy, then only two years old. There was a daughter, also named Annie, who had an illegitimate son and then married a young sailor who unfortunately was killed during the war in a bomb attack on Plymouth Docks. Young Annie was pregnant at the time, ultimately giving birth to a daughter, and the last I heard of her was that she married a GI named Narozniak, and the whole mixed brood went to live in the States. She shared her mother's sense of humour, and I vividly remember her telling a story about an acquaintance of hers who had a rather large family to which she added while her husband was away in the navy. When asked how she accounted for the extra offspring on her husband's return she said, 'Why, he just sat up at table with t'others, and 'e never saw no difference!'

Anyone familiar with Dawlish will know that one abiding feature of the town is an ornamental garden, divided by a stream that descends through small waterfalls, from what used to be the inland outskirts right down to its outlet under a railway viaduct into the sea. For many years, during the summer season, there was a large marquee in these gardens housing a twice-nightly concert party, a visit to which was always a holiday highlight. There were usually an over-the-hill baritone and an ageing soprano with pronounced vibrato, but thankfully the bill was always topped by a marvellous comedian. He would appear in sketches throughout the show, and then do his own solo spot. I remember one of them doing a sort of pantomime dame drag act which he started with the line, 'Do you like me dress? I cut it out meself with a knife and fork.' Irresistibly funny to a seven year old boy.

Beside these gardens, or 'The Lawn', as they were known, was the office of the local charabanc proprietor, one Mr Hopkins, a moustachioed worthy who stood outside his premises in a blazer, wing collar, and a sort of yachtsman's peaked cap. His splendid vehicle was a convertible coach, the like of which is never seen today, and in it one could make trips to Buckfast Abbey, to Babbacombe, or up on to Dartmoor. In fact the week's holiday was quite deliberately planned around special events: the motorboat trip, the variety show and Hopkins' tours. Did the sun shine every day I wonder? It certainly does in my memory.

At ten, I was unaware of the approach of World War Two; it arrived at exactly the time that I transferred to grammar school. There were two of these for boys and two for girls in Coventry in 1939. Boys had the choice of King Henry VIII and Bablake. My parents chose the latter for me. It was a school founded by a wealthy merchant, Thomas Wheatley, in the fifteenth century; the original black and white timbered building, converted to a hostelry for male pensioners, survived the blitzkrieg attacks which virtually demolished the centre of the city.

My first months at Bablake were strange indeed, for this was a period of calm before the storm. The school operated what it called a tutorial system, whereby we attended mornings only for a couple of days a week and collected set work intended for study at home. Then came the first blitz on Coventry, and shortly afterwards the whole school was evacuated *en masse* to Lincoln. Some boys were housed in hostels, supervised by housemasters, but most of us were placed with private families in billets. Our main school was a conglomeration of corrugated iron huts which had been a military hospital during the previous war, and for classes that needed special facilities, such as chemistry, physics or art, we were generously accommodated in local boys' and girls' secondary schools.

It always struck me as faintly odd that Lincoln was chosen as a haven for our school, situated as it was amidst no fewer than four or five RAF aerodromes that might have been supposed to be prime targets, although I don't recall any bombs falling in the area during the three years that I lived there.

One of the prime attractions of my new home was a pool known as the Braford. Surrounded by corn warehouses and an agricultural machinery factory, it was on a confluence of the river Witham and the Fossdyke canal. One side of this pool was lined by a variety of craft used for the most part as houseboats; one of these in particular was the home of a sturdy elderly lady who used to rent us her tender on the agreement that she would teach us to row properly. I've never ceased to be grateful to her. Much less wisely, one or two of us occasionally joined a bunch of local toughs in diving off a swing bridge and swimming through the highly polluted waters to a small island in the middle of the pool. It's a wonder we survived.

The first lady with whom I was billeted was a Mrs Cope who had three young children of her own and whose husband was an army sergeant serving overseas. Despite the fact that she lived in a small terraced house with a tiny shop that was closed for the duration of the war she nevertheless took in three of us and we all slept in an unexpected four poster bed in the back bedroom. Mrs Cope was a kind, caring and truly motherly woman who gave us affection as well as shelter.

Her brother, I remember, ran a large poultry farm in the Fen district. He was a handsome man, but ineligible for military service as he had lost an arm in an accident on a threshing machine, and then a thumb on his remaining hand. For all that, he drove a car, ran

[27]

his farm almost on his own, and was an expert with a shot-gun. I was taken to this farm during one school holiday and for the first time in my life saw pork in a brine tub in the vast kitchen and home-cured ham hanging from the beams. I helped collect the eggs each day and learned how to weigh them, selecting those large enough for hatching in the incubators, and eventually experiencing the magic of watching the young chicks emerge from their shells.

One experience I didn't enjoy was worse even than watching my friend John Johnson's father slaughter chickens. I was taken, all unsuspecting, to watch a pig being killed in the most primitive way imaginable. The poor animal was tethered by its snout and by its legs, then the butcher straddled the creature and cut its throat. As the squealing, weakening beast fell on to its side he then knelt on it and pumped the remaining blood from the wound. Finally buckets of boiling water were thrown over the carcase and the hairs scraped from it before it was dismembered. I hope such brutality has long since been outlawed.

An aspect of life with the Cope family that I recall with special pleasure is that I would go with them every week to the Theatre Royal, then a home for the occasional touring show, but usually for twice-nightly variety. This bijou Regency theatre was all gilt and red plush in the stalls and circle, but we were patrons of the gallery at an admission charge of, I think, tuppence, and sat on the boards which lined the concrete steps of this top shelf. In that theatre I saw Tom Walls and Ralph Lynn in *Rookery Nook*, the amazing striptease queen Phyllis Dixey with her innocuous impressions of nude paintings such as *September Morn* and *Love Looked Out* interspersed with her much naughtier monologues.

It's a wonder that, with so many extra-curricular diversions, I managed to get through enough school work to pass what was known in those days as the School Certificate and so qualify to pass into the senior school and the sixth form, but I did. At that point evacuation was no longer considered necessary and Bablake School returned to Coventry. Not before I had taken part in a school concert, however, at which I caused a minor sensation by performing two George Formby songs, 'When I'm Cleaning Windows' and 'Chinese Laundry Blues'; I played the ukelele and sang, accompanied by two classmates on bones!

The return to Coventry should have been marked by a more dedicated approach to the work which could gain me a place at university, for about this time all those early years of chapel and Sunday school had brainwashed me into thinking that I wanted to be a parson. This idea persisted for two or three years, but not strongly enough to divert me from more hedonistic pleasures.

The war of course was still in progress and most of us were by that time anticipating military service of some kind between school and university. This in itself was no great inducement to academic effort; moreover, many of the younger teachers were themselves in the forces which meant that those who were left, for reasons of either health or age, were often very much second division. For a short spell – unprecedently – a woman teacher was taken on to the staff, but comically, no acknowledgement of her sex was permitted: her name was never used, she appeared on our timetables as Number Seven and in class we were instructed to address her as 'Sir'. Now, I can scarcely believe this yet it is entirely true. It was a doubly strange policy for a headmaster of great sophistication, refinement and wisdom; it simply reflects the appalling sexist attitudes and the segregation prevalent in education in the first half of this century.

The aforementioned headmaster was one W.E. Seaborne, who spoke in the manner of the older Winston Churchill and with something of that political historian's command of and relish for resounding English. For example, to those of us newly promoted to the awesome responsibility of prefects: 'The only way to run a school successfully is as an enlightened dictator. That is what I am. You are my lieutenants.' Another comment was about my appearance when, newly demobbed from the army and enrolled at RADA, I made what I thought was a triumphant return to the scene of my academic failures. The deputy headmaster, a blunt Yorkshireman, had remarked that I looked as if I could do with an 'aircut. Seaborne retorted, 'Oh, come Mr Atkins. You must allow

[29]

him the badge of his profession!'

A language master who had a profound and lasting effect on me, despite the fact that during the time we knew each other I was to him a source of irritation, frustration and ultimately blistering rage, was Frank Barter, wondrously nick-named Bonk. He was a linguist of outstanding brilliance; his total fluency in French, German, Spanish and no doubt other European tongues was firmly founded on a thorough knowledge of Latin and Greek. His great subject was etymology and he constantly cross-referenced the origins of words; this eventually filtered through to me as a splendid way to learn and understand any language. He also insisted on conducting his classes in whichever language they happened to be about and if you had the temerity to address him in English he would thunder, 'When I pay you the compliment of addressing you in . . . (French, German or whatever) you will have the courtesy to answer me in the same language.' His method clearly worked, for I passed the Higher School Certificate in French and German almost entirely on the oral parts of the examination.

Bonk Barter, a lifelong bachelor, also had a strong streak of cruelty which I am sad to say seemed an all too common characteristic among masters during my time at school. Few could resist the temptation to hold the weaker intellects among us up to ridicule to extract cheap laughs from their classmates.

There was, for example, a chemistry teacher whose chief delight was to keep some poor chap on his feet stumbling over formulae that he couldn't grasp. 'Give me the equation for the action of sulphuric acid on copper sulphate,' he would sneer. Then after much fruitless prodding and probing would come the line the rest of us were all gleefully awaiting, 'Really! I could teach an intelligent puppy that in a fortnight.' Uncontrolled mirth from twenty-nine little creeps only too pleased that they had not been the butt of the cynicism. I'm ashamed to admit I was all too often of their number, but what, I have wondered ever since, of the poor blushing lad, sweating and tongue-tied?

I had one really vicious enemy myself whose animosity I still find hard to understand. He had been a prefect when I was a second former and due to some physical defect was unable to enter the forces. He therefore went straight to university and then came back to Bablake to join the severely depleted teaching staff as another sixth form French master. We took an instant dislike to each other but he, of course, had the power. His unkindest ploy was to slash red pencil marks through my translations despite the fact that they were no different from those of my colleagues, and consequently giving me the lowest marks possible. This resulted on more than one occasion in my being sent to detention to sit, as a prefect, among second and third formers who had been indicted for smoking in the bogs, or cycling on hallowed ground.

How strange that that particular memory should surface now, having lain dormant for forty years or more. My resentment must certainly have gone deep, and it is with a degree of childish satisfaction that I now remember the spiteful French teacher's name was, strangely appropriately, Malin.

Happiness came during those years mainly from out-of-school activities and chiefly from cycling. My best friend was Bert Bower; while still evacuated to Lincoln we cycled the seventy-five miles home to Coventry for one holiday and later joined the Youth Hostels Association which enabled us, during the next few years, to tour many parts of England and Wales at very small cost. There were few motor vehicles on the roads, due to petrol rationing; in that respect at least we were lucky to spend our teenage years during the war.

By the time I had reached the age of seventeen I had begun to have grave doubts about entering the church, partly because I had started to find it boring, but much more because I had fallen in love with a girl who had no doubt at all that she was going to be an actress. On a weekend hostelling trip to Cleeve Hill Bert and I shared a dormitory with a bearded lecturer in philosophy. This opportunity for guidance was too good to miss, so I laid my dilemma before him: the church or the stage? He rather unhelpfully answered that my problem was not surprising, since they both had numerous similarities. Of course he was right, but I must say that although I have subsequently met several clerics who might make splendid actors I can't recall any actors of merit who might grace the cloth.

There was one area in which school and outside activities crossed rather pleasantly. Our orchestra lacked a trombone player and so I volunteered for the chair, confident that my father would be able to tutor me to some degree of proficiency, and indeed he did. Our two specialities were Elgar's 'Pomp and Circumstance Number Two' and the 'Grasshoppers' Dance' by Boccherini; both were churned out at one or two school concerts. But best of all, the first clarinet, whose name was Jackson, had discovered jazz and had even learned from records to play some of Benny Goodman's easier licks. His enthusiasm was caught by the first trumpet, Stan Wright, and they enlisted me on trombone. Who else we brought in I have no idea, but we used to gather in a sort of Dixieland outfit on summer Sunday evenings in Coventry's Memorial Park where we played countless choruses of 'Muskrat Ramble'. Badly. And very loud.

By this time Mum and Dad had forsaken their beloved Dawlish for summer holidays largely because the beaches were covered in rolls of barbed wire to hinder the expected German invasion. They went instead to Stratford-on-Avon for one or two weeks, during which time it was in those days possible to see, at the Shakespeare Memorial Theatre, all of the plays in the repertoire, usually six by the bard and one other by Johnson or Goldsmith. The company was always led from the front by an actor manager and I count myself lucky to have seen the legendary Robert Atkins, later renowned for his open air seasons in Regent's Park, and Anthony Quayle, before the university boys took over and turned it all into director's theatre and the Royal Shakespeare Company.

Memories of Stratford in the nineteen forties are perhaps filtered through rose-coloured glasses, but I am convinced that there was a special magic about seeing a magnificent actor like Abraham Sofaer perform Lear one night and Malvolio the next. Margaretta Scott as Portia delivered the 'quality of mercy' speech as I have never heard

A Salvation Army outing from Eccles, c. 1890. My father is second from the right, front row

Left: My father, a budding Salvation Army bandsman, with my Gran. *Right*: Mum and Dad's wedding, 1926

My own wedding, 1951. The small bridesmaid, Pamela's second cousin, now has children of her own

Left: Is this my unnamed grandfather? He certainly resembles . . . (*right*) . . . my father

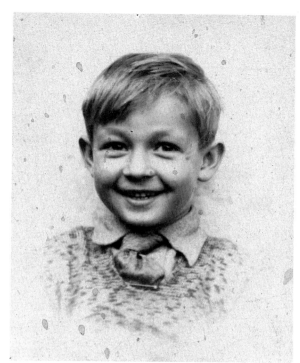

This is certainly me, aged 5 . . .

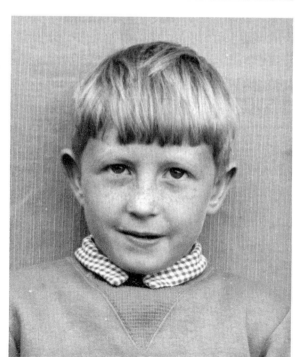

. . . and this my son Christopher, aged 6

Left: Boats have always been a passion. This was the first — 'Uncle' Frank's trip-boat in Dawlish. I was barely two. *Right*: On the clifftops at Dawlish, with Mum

Left: At Brixham with Mum and Dad, 1937. *Right*: Salcombe, Devon, 1939 with Mum and my best friend John Johnson

Early radio days. BFN Hamburg, 1948

Left: RADA students, 1950. The acrobat was that fine comedy actor, the late Derek Royle.
Right: From the BBC's files: Brian Matthew, BBC announcer, General Division (London)
26.6.58

In Fécamp harbour with *Espada*

The first small sailing boat *Chrisje*

The first *Round Midnight* – 27 ft

. . . and the next, a bit bigger . . .

. . . and the last, bigger and better
still

Introducing 'Saturday Club'

it since, and as Hermione in *A Winter's Tale* had a truly breath-taking statuesque beauty.

The days, which of course were always brilliantly sunny, were spent on the river, then happily devoid of plastic motor cruisers, and I was able to show off my rowing skills as taught by the lady on the Braford in Lincoln, and to learn the much more dangerous art of poling a punt. In some respects the punt was better, because it was possible to get much further upstream by jumping over the side and handling it through a series of shallow rapids. It was on one such occasion that I saw for the first time a kingfisher sitting in one of the riverside bushes.

I also remember, with a frisson of delight, poling a punt through Clopton bridge in a rather strong cross wind. A bunch of lads hung over the parapet jeering at my efforts, but were stopped short in their tracks by the boatyard proprietor who shouted up to them, 'When you can 'andle a boat 'alf as well as 'e's doin', you'll 'ave summat to shout about.'

World War Two came to an end a year before I had finished school. My trumpet playing friend, Stan Wright, and I were on a walking holiday in the Black Mountains of South Wales when the final victory over Japan was announced. We swam naked in the fast-running river Usk, got drunk and ill on some evil farmhouse-brewed rough cider and discovered the much more satisfactory intoxication of sitting alone on a mountain top reading aloud from Ruskin's *Sesame and Lilies* convinced that we understood every word. Oh, the blissful unwitting pretentiousness of youth.

One strange little hostel in that part of the world was deep in a valley at Capel y Ffin. The warden was a monk, Father David, who belonged to an order which required its brethren to spend some of their time in lay jobs. He was a very strange man who sat up late one night by oil lamp telling us amazing tales of how he had mastered the secrets of astral projection so that his astral body could undertake journeys while his earthly body lay asleep. On a more mundane level he told us that he took a shower every morning under a waterfall behind the hostel. Stan and I felt that we could hardly be less macho than this holy man, so we left our bunks early in the morning and stood beneath the mountain stream waterfall until we were breathless and blue. Then Father David arrived, threw off his habit, strode into the water, and straight out again. And maybe that was when I lost a little more of my former faith.

[3]

The end of hostilities in 1945 did not mean the end of military service. For several years to come all able-bodied youths of eighteen were obliged to enlist in one of the armed forces for a period of two years.

There are still people today who believe that was a good and worthwhile policy. It broadened the lads' outlook, they say. It made men of them. I do not in any way subscribe to these ideas and can only deplore the waste of two years spent in an environment in which the daily tools were instruments of death. However, as things were to turn out a little later in my life, I have to admit that they were to some extent made possible by my army service.

School ended for me in June 1946; I successfully passed the Higher School Certificate in English, French, German, History and Economics, and I was offered a Bablake scholarship should I take up a place at theological college after my military service. I never had the benefit of that scholarship, since by the time of demobilisation I had chosen to worship at a different shrine.

For a few weeks I was taken on at Centaur Road school, where I had started, as a supervisor of large classes of unruly little monsters. The experience went some small way towards helping me to understand the cruelty and cynicism of teachers; up until then I had only been on the receiving end.

In September I reached the age of eighteen and received my call up papers; my beloved left for London and RADA. There was a tearful farewell on Coventry Station, but how quickly we both got over it!

Less than a month later I reported for duty at, by coincidence,

Lincoln Barracks for six weeks preliminary training. Our squad of thirty was a very mixed bag indeed; it included a few men older than the rest of us who had been 'Bevin boys'. They had been working in the coal mines under a scheme introduced by Ernest Bevin whereby it was possible to opt for service in the pits rather than the forces. There must have been some sort of get out clause which enabled them, at a later stage, to change their minds and go into the army after all. Most of these chaps were very hard men indeed and prodigious drinkers to boot, consuming as many as fifteen or sixteen pints on pay day. They also volunteered for the optional boxing training, which was rewarded with an extra weekend pass, and at the eventual battalion contest they achieved some pretty impressive knock-outs.

During the first few days there were one or two attempts to gain dismissal from the forces to 'work your ticket' as it was called, but I only saw one man succeed. His finest stroke came when we were ordered to blanco our kit. Blanco was a khaki block of powder which, mixed with water, was applied to belts, gaiters, packs and all items made of webbing. This bright spark did indeed blanco his kit, including his greatcoat, boots and underwear. On the day he left us, designated unfit for military training, there was a good deal more wisdom than witlessness in the smile he bestowed on the rest of us.

As many people writing about those days of conscription have recorded, an odd aspect of training required constant changes of clothing in record-breaking time. Thus, on returning from the cook-house, the order might be, 'Everybody outside in denims, double quick!' And no sooner had we assembled outside our hut than the corporal would bellow, 'Right, on the command "Dismiss" everybody inside and back out here in your number one uniform in two minutes.' But ours had a refinement up his sleeve. We each had two pairs of boots: one for square bashing and rough work and one 'best', boned and polished with toecaps like mirrors, reserved for ceremonial parades. Our own resident masochist ordered us to report in denim fatigues, then marched us to a store to collect picks and shovels, back to our barrack rooms to change into our best

[36]

boots and then out to a field of mud to dig slit trenches, thus ruining weeks of 'bull' (polishing) and leaving precious little time to restore a shine before our passing out parade.

We learned to clean our rifles and even on rare occasions how to fire them: we were taught to dismantle and reassemble Bren machine guns, and we marched and drilled until we were almost asleep on our feet. We were herded into a windowless brick-built structure which turned out to be a maze of knee-high tunnels and left to find our way out as quickly as possible while tear gas was blown into the interior.

After six weeks of this deliberate madness we were deemed to be trained soldiers and sent either to our units, or to other centres for further training. I was in a small group despatched to Hilsea Barracks in Portsmouth to be taught to be a clerk in the Ordnance Corps, the army's supply unit; there were vast depots all over the place stuffed with clothing, furniture, and other commodities for the domestic side of military life. This course lasted for a month during which we were all required on at least one occasion to mount guard at the barrack gates. Opposite those gates was a café; on the night that I was a member of the guard thieves broke in and cleaned the place out. One of us must surely have witnessed the offence, but none of us had, and I wonder to this day whether it occurred while I nodded off in the middle of the night in my sentry box.

At the end of our clerical training, three or four of us were sent to Salisbury Plain for our first encounter with a military bungle. By this time the worst winter in living memory was just starting, and we arrived to find that nobody expected us; there was no accommodation for us and nothing for us to do. We were found beds and given meals; we were then told to spend our days out of the way in a blanket store, where at least it was warm, until somebody decided what to do with us.

My main friend at this time was known as 'Fido' Fallows; he had been in Lincoln and Portsmouth with me. He was small, dark and handsome; he was one of the few people in our midst already engaged to be married. He always returned from weekend leave a seething mass of neuroses; his betrothed apparently refused to allow him to have his way with her. Fido it was, one bitterly cold night, who introduced me in the local pub to the comforts of mulled ale; we sat heating a poker red-hot in the open fire then plunging it into our pints. That was to prove the first of many occasions when we tottered back to barracks much the worse for wear.

After a couple of weeks on Salisbury Plain a few of us were posted to Number Five Ordnance Depot at Branston, Burton-on-Trent, which was to prove my home for the next year. Although there were spells of brain numbing tedium spent filling in stock forms, inevitably in triplicate, there were also times of great enjoyment.

The early part of 1947 saw Britain in the grip of the most severe winter in living memory, the like of which has not been experienced since. There were temperatures of more than twenty degrees below zero and much of the country was snowbound. Branston became a centre for a huge operation, code named King Coal, during which RASC drivers were attached to our unit, going out daily with lorry loads of fuel and other essential supplies. These drivers became a source of envy, since they were given a daily rum ration and issued with wonderful leather jerkins not available to the rest of us.

During this period I shared a Nissen hut with eight or ten other chaps, and we never knew what it was to be warm. The only heating came from a central stove fired with a ration of coke and any other combustible we could lay our hands on. Much army furniture 'mysteriously' disappeared at this time and months later, when I had become an acting quarter-master, I was called upon by the commanding officer to account for 'tables, telegraph, two hundred' which were on our inventory but not in our billets. I knew where they had gone and I suspect he knew as well, but nevertheless fictitious documents had to be produced to explain the deficiency convincingly.

The great character in this depot was a Regimental Sergeant Major of splendid physique who spoke with a broad Devonshire accent. He had a warm sense of humour but he was addicted to discipline. His active service record was impressive and he commanded a strange mixture of respect and fear not only among the other ranks, but also among junior subalterns fresh from public school with no active service record at all. On pay parades, this Sergeant Major would announce the latest orders and then roar, 'If I find anyone failing to follow these instructions I'll 'ave 'im. From the 'ighest', a crushing glance round the second lieutenants, 'to the bloody lowest', a fearsome look that quelled the rest of us, 'I'll 'ave 'im.'

There were occasional drill parades conducted by this RSM to prevent those of us who had settled for the sedentary roles of clerks becoming too soft, but they always reminded me of performances by a vulgar but well-liked stand-up comedian. 'Look at that back rank,' he would bark. 'Look at it. About as straight as my prick on a Monday morning.'

Another man who had control over my life at this time was a Captain Webber who sat in solitary splendour in an office in the centre of the huge clothing warehouse to which I reported every day to fill in the aforementioned forms in triplicate. Now since this didn't occupy too much of my time I fell into a habit of drawing cartoons of some of the civilians employed by the RAOC, and inevitably some of these sketches found their way on to the walls of other offices, to the chagrin, understandably, of the principal butt of the jokes. He contented himself at first with mumbling comments such as 'Ought to be in the bloody artists' rifles, you ought,' but was eventually driven to complain to Captain Webber. Fortunately for me this officer had the wisdom to see that what I was doing stemmed more from boredom than from malice, and instead of punishing me he threw at me the Army Manual of Touch Typing, guided me to a typewriter in an office all to myself and said, 'Now, get on with that.'

I may not have learned terribly well and I don't pretend to be fast, but in all my years as a broadcaster with countless scripts behind me I have never ceased to be grateful to that captain.

Rather sadly, these two men were destined to become involved in an all too familiar scenario which reflected no credit on either of them. In those days the haven of all squaddies at army units was the NAAFI canteen where the inadequacies of the mess could be supplemented with cheap snacks and cups of tea and where we drew our cigarette ration. In the spring of 1947 there came to our particular oasis a manageress considered by many to be of great beauty; she was clearly modelled on one or two of the screen goddesses of the period. She wore very heavy make-up and trailed, I recall, a dense cloud of potent if cheap perfume.

The Captain and the RSM were both totally smitten and set out to obtain the lady's favours. Unfortunately it would seem that they both succeeded and thereby gave the lie to the old adage that Hell hath no fury like a woman scorned. That fury fades into insignificance beside the fury of the two men who have both been anything but scorned by the same woman. In this instance, alas, they fell to blows all too publicly and for those of you unfamiliar with the rules of the army game it must be pointed out that there are worse crimes than striking a commissioned officer, but not many. When the striker happens to be a warrant officer himself he might well echo Hamlet's stepfather, Claudius, 'O, my offence is rank!'

The RSM was immediately relieved of duties and confined to barracks. This once fine figure of a man lost weight perceptibly and in all respects became a mere shadow of his former self; he was no doubt aware that he had squandered his record and reputation. Both he and Captain Webber were eventually transferred elsewhere.

My own free time activities now centred once again on theatrical matters. I discovered that Burton Education Authority had established a drama school in the town with a few full time students and evening classes for part timers. I enrolled immediately and took part in a production of the famous comedy *The Man Who Came To Dinner*.

I also became deeply enamoured of a glamorous young woman who was a member of the part time classes and who turned out to be the daughter of a widow who was the landlady of the Rose and Crown in Burton. Some of my army colleagues thought I had found the crock of gold at the end of the rainbow and indeed for a while I felt very like that myself before I was superseded by a more mature and attractive commercial traveller.

While so much of my free time was spent savouring the greasepaint and the fleshpots, not to mention many a free libation, I probably failed to travel home to Coventry as often as I might, but I did enter a competition there for which the first prize was a scholarship to the London Academy of Music and Dramatic Art. My audition piece was the dagger speech from *Macbeth* and, although I can now imagine how horrendously over the top it may very well have been, I did do well enough to get into the finals. And then the blow fell. I was drafted to Germany. My commanding officer expressed sympathy but could find no reason to help me out of the problem. At the age of nineteen I felt as though it was the end of the world and that my career was over before it had begun. Of course there was no way I could know that I was about to take the first steps towards a profession that was to occupy most of my life for the next forty years.

[4]

Until the early part of 1948 I had never set foot outside Britain and despite my disappointment over missing the finals of the acting competition I looked forward to my posting to the British Army of the Rhine as a war substantive fully paid corporal. As a regular listener to the Sunday radio programme 'Two Way Family Favourites', presented in those days by Sergeant Derek Jones in Hamburg and Jean Metcalfe in London, I had already made up my mind that I wanted to be posted to the British Forces Network.

The actual journey is nothing more than a blur in my memory. We were first assembled at a barracks in Felsted, then taken by train to Harwich for a night time embarkation to the Hook of Holland. Then there was a train ride through the Netherlands and into Germany and finally we climbed wearily into trucks for transport to an old German barracks in the town of Bielefeld. But if the details of that journey are hazy in my mind, my first night in Bielefeld is etched indelibly by a bizarre chain of events.

First, to my total amazement, I found myself detailed as guard commander at the main gate, which lay on a road running out of the town. So there I was, in a foreign country, in a totally unfamiliar environment, commanding a guard of men I'd never met in my life. The orders were explicit and strict. I was at all times to be fully dressed, although we were in shirt-sleeve order, and fully armed. In addition to visiting all sentries at prescribed intervals I also had to inspect an ammunition store in the basement of a block.

The first shock for this very green corporal, nineteen years old, came well before midnight with a series of piercing screams somewhere outside the guardroom followed by a sentry bellowing,

[42]

'Guard Commander!' On rushing out to investigate, I found a young soldier pointing his rifle at a quivering German couple who stood, hands in the air, gibbering '*Kamerad, Kamerad.*'

It was then that I discovered my Higher Schools Certificate German bore precious little resemblance to the language spoken at least by the inhabitants of Bielefeld. However, it sufficed to elicit that this couple had been visiting their family in the town and had stayed late, missing the curfew imposed on all civilians. I was also just about able to calm their terror, which was probably only a shade more acute than that of the sentry and myself.

Some time later, on one of my checks of the unlit underground ammunition store, my heart stopped again when I felt the point of a blade dragged along my bare forearm and then a warm trickle of blood. When I found the courage to shine a torch on my 'assailant' I discovered with great relief that it was no more than a sharp piece of metal sticking out of the wall.

The final excitement occurred when a member of the guard rushed in demanding my assistance outside the sergeants' mess. I accompanied him back and found a diminutive RSM lying apparently comatose in a pool of schnapps, beer and his own vomit. On my approach he leapt to his feet and ran off with me in hot pursuit into a barrack block and up several flights of stairs. He opened the door to a room, then turned on me in all his drunken blazing rage and screamed, 'I'll bloody have you for this, corporal. I'll have your bloody stripes and your bloody life.'

On returning to the guard room I discovered a right little Job's comforter: a demented orderly whose own overdue demobilisation would seem to have been delayed by someone with a strong sense of sympathy for the great British public. He assured me that I'd really done it this time and would undoubtedly be, as he was himself, detained indefinitely in Bielefeld pending further enquiries. Fortunately he proved to be ill informed on this matter and the next day I was posted to an Ordnance Depot in a rural spot called Glinde some fifteen kilometres outside Hamburg.

My first move was to request an audition for Forces Radio, or rather the BFN. I was temporarily attached to a friendly quartermaster sergeant's office where I had absolutely nothing to do whatsoever. The audition came up quickly enough and my application was successful. I learned later that I had been described as 'too BBC' by the head of presentation, who was, in later years, to achieve considerable celebrity himself with the television programme 'Tomorrow's World'. His name was Raymond Baxter.

Fortunately for me another member of the panel was a sergeant, Trevor Hill, who was destined to become an outstanding drama producer for the BBC in Manchester, and he argued that it would be no bad thing to have someone at the station with the BBC style of that time. Trevor won the day and I passed the audition, but I was not to find this out for some time and so was left to kick my heels in Glinde for a further five months.

Situated as we were in a country district, one of the leisure options available to us was riding lessons under the tuition of a former German cavalry instructor. He sent me out first of all on a huge animal that galloped off into the heather and then set about doing everything it could to throw me. Realising that I knew nothing at all, the cavalryman then took me into the paddock and tried to teach me how to sit and how to grip with my knees. The next day I could scarcely walk and that, sadly, was the end of my attempt to learn to ride.

On another occasion my friendly quartermaster sent me out with a German driver and a truck carrying rolls of blankets ostensibly bound for a laundry. In fact, unknown to me, tins of ration chocolate were wrapped in the blankets. We visited a civilian house miles from the depot and there exchanged the chocolate for two bottles of illicitly distilled hooch, one labelled 'Kirsch' and the other 'Whiskey' in German handwriting. Both were colourless liquids; this was my one and only encounter with the highly dangerous local moonshine, wood alcohol.

On my return to base, the quartermaster and I despatched the greater part of this stuff and he was thus inspired to suggest a trip into Hamburg for a visit to a bar in the Ratskeller only open to sergeants and above. He said there was no need to worry as he would lend me one of his jackets with its three stripes. Happily someone was watching over me as the route back to my billet lay round, or as it turned out in my case, through an assault course, with ditches, fences, barbed-wire entanglements and all, and by the time I had negotiated the lot I passed out on my cot for several hours.

The least happy memories of this period in Glinde stemmed from the fact that I was the non-commissioned officer in charge of a barrack room of some thirty or so bored and reluctant men. My instructions were to ensure that they were at all times properly dressed and always wore their berets when leaving for the mess. An early attempt to enforce this regulation resulted in a vulgar expletive from one man; I had no alternative but to put him on a charge. He came up before the commanding officer, who for some obscure reason, considering the trivial nature of the offence, remanded the poor chap for the brigadier.

Although I regret this episode, there was one bizarre moment to relish. The brigadier, it transpired, was an archetypal brass hat although he was youngish for such an exalted rank. He listened to the charge, and to my account of the incident. He then questioned me as to the dialogue that had ensued. He asked me sternly, 'And what did the soldier reply, corporal?'

'Bollocks, sir,' was the only truthful answer I could give.

Not my least reason for hating the army pomposity of the time is that, for this small misdemeanour, the accused was sentenced to a month in the glasshouse, the barrack prison.

That night one of his mates over indulged in the NAAFI and after lights out almost incited the great Glinde mutiny. 'My mucker,' he cried, 'he's in the nick. All down to that bastard corporal.' He was right. Cold sweat broke out down my back. 'Let's get the bastard,' he screamed.

It was a nasty dangerous moment.

'Shut up,' I snapped, 'or you'll find yourself inside with him.'

Thankfully he did shut up and the moment passed, but the fact

[45]

that I remember it so graphically more than forty years later indicates the guilt that I felt.

Happily, a little later I discovered that my posting to BFN in Hamburg had been authorised, but had been carelessly left unattended in some orderly room clerk's 'In' tray. Matters were soon cleared up and I packed my kitbag and left for the great world of broadcasting. Things were looking up at last.

[5]

Hamburg in 1948 was an impoverished, half-ruined city where the citizens were for the most part poorly clad and ill-fed. Galloping inflation had left the mark practically worthless and much trading went on by means of barter. Sad faced Germans stood about regularly outside the Hauptbahnhof, clutching some once treasured possession or other, hoping to swap it with someone from the British forces for chocolate or cigarettes.

All that was left of the former grandiose Opera House was the part of the building which had originally been the stage, though performances were still given in this restricted space.

It was possible to rent rowing boats on the city's famous lake, the Alster, but stories of decomposing limbs rising to the surface on the blades of the oars were common.

The most prized jobs for the civilians were with the occupation forces, for at least they provided some albeit modest income and the possibility of obtaining food. Outside working hours fraternisation was discouraged by military authorities but in a rather half-hearted way, so that amateur prostitution was far from rare.

The headquarters were in the large and undamaged Konzerthalle which had belonged to the Nordwest Deutscherundfunk; the studios and offices for broadcasting were there. Our living accommodation was a mile or two away in the commandeered Hotel Zum Kronprinz, opposite Hamburg's other railway station, the Sudbahnhof. This was a dramatic and welcome change after a year and a half spent in barracks and, although there was an army captain with a small administration staff to keep up the pretence that this was still a military unit, we lived and felt like civilians in an exciting, stimulating atmosphere.

The highest standards of professionalism were always sought and maintained on air with a constant vigilant watch kept on the performances; any evidence of slipshod work was dealt with immediately. On my arrival at the station I was summoned to Raymond Baxter's office for a welcome and a brief rundown on what might be expected of me. He was a handsome, debonair figure with an aura of the archetypal *Boy's Own* hero. Though by this time a civilian he still carried the air of the RAF pilot that I believe he had been. As I was to discover later, he also had a glamorous American wife and, to top it all, he drove an MG sports car.

He spoke, I recall, with a rather more languorous drawl than he uses today and he ended his address by saying, 'Rape, pillage, murder and theft we'll do our best to cover up. There's just one thing that will not be tolerated under any circumstances, and that's going on air drunk.'

The talent that had been assembled by BFN was awe-inspiring and many of the young unknowns who were my colleagues have gone on to distinguished careers in radio, television and entertainment generally. George Melachrino conducted the orchestra; on fourth clarinet, so he confessed to me in a television studio many years later, was Bert Kaempfert. The head of the Variety Department was Cliff Michelmore who, during my months at the station, himself took over the Hamburg end of 'Family Favourites' and eventually married the London presenter, Jean Metcalfe. Our chief announcer was Nigel Davenport, who is now a well-known actor and President of Equity. He had succeeded Sergeant Robin Boyle who had been demobbed but came back for a spell as a civilian just before I left; also on the announcing staff at that time was Tim Gudgin.

The drama producer Trevor Hill whom I mentioned earlier shared an office with the only woman among the personnel, a WAAF sergeant named Margaret Potter who wrote scripts. They too married eventually and continued their professional partnership for the BBC in Manchester. One of the jobs that many of us enjoyed enormously was recording a dramatic serial they had created between them: 'The Adventures of Robin Hood'. Nigel Davenport was Robin and I played King Richard. A few years later Trevor repeated the series for the BBC and on that occasion I played a role he wrote in for me because the King had already been cast: Sir Simon Gray, 'a knight with a commanding air'.

One other BFN staff member I must mention was an RAF corporal who worked in the gramophone library. His great ambition was to buy a handmade guitar and although he was a heavy smoker he gave it up, selling his cigarette ration to raise funds. We had no German currency at that time; we were paid in a sort of monopoly money known as BAFS, which consisted of plastic pennies and halfpennies, while everything from the denomination of threepence upwards was in paper money. How this librarian managed to exchange his BAFS for marks I never discovered, but sure enough the day came when he proudly brought back to the hotel a beautiful shining instrument. In later years I used to persuade myself that my own addiction to the weed had played some small part in launching the career of the father of British blues, Alexis Korner.

By this time I had completely made up my mind that I wanted to be an actor on returning to civvy street, so I set about arranging an audition for RADA and getting the government grant available to those whose education had been interrupted by conscription. I expected to be released in October 1948, but before that could happen there was a Russian blockade of Berlin and all demobilisation was suspended for at least three months. The good news was that, unlike universities, RADA accepted new students each term and not just once a year so that if I was successful I could hope to start in January 1949.

Meanwhile, as Christmas 1948 approached, we were visited by a director of the spoken word from BBC London, David Lloyd James, whose father had composed one of the broadcaster's bibles; a pronunciation dictionary. He asked some of us if we would be interested in a career with the BBC after demob and I declined

[49]

rather pompously, saying that I was going to go on the stage. David also auditioned a handful of announcers to choose one of us to introduce an orchestral programme from Hamburg to be broadcast live on Christmas morning on the BBC Light Programme, and I was the lucky one.

In an old box of letters that came my way when my mother died I found a letter to me from my father that he wrote to me on Boxing Day 1948. 'Sincere congratulations,' he wrote. 'You did the job splendidly. When we heard the London announcer say, "A Merry Christmas, Brian Matthew" it was a thrill the like of which I had never experienced. Then came your voice true and clear, and I wanted to jump and to dance and to cry all at once.'

After that broadcast I walked back to the Hotel Zum Kronprinz for our Christmas dinner. Soon after leaving the studio I was accosted by a prostitute standing in a doorway. Some of these Hamburg ladies wore a sort of uniform at that time, consisting of a short cape and a pointed hat, rather like a witch's, so I had no doubt about what she was. As I passed she said softly in a Dietrich sort of voice, '*Komm mit mir.*' To which I replied in some confusion, 'No thank you,' whereupon she laughed and laughed.

Another strange memory of Hamburg is of a Church Army canteen which occupied a rather pleasant first floor café where a German string quartet entertained us; they would play requests in return for a few cigarettes. This building also housed a lift system the like of which I had never seen before: two openings, one for up and one for down, no doors and a constantly moving sequence of platforms, so that one had to jump in and out pretty nippily. But what, we wondered, happened to those lifts at the top and the bottom of the building? Did they turn over completely, or did they collapse flat to go round the turn? There was only one way to find out and of course we never had the bottle to try. Not until some years later, that is, when I went back to Hamburg with a BBC team for a live broadcast. I took some friends to the building, and lo and behold the lifts were still there. Two of us jumped in and waited rather nervously, in total darkness, to see what happened after the top floor. To our intense relief, the lift stayed upright, moved to the side and started to descend.

The colleague with whom I shared a hotel room while with BFN was a splendid friend with a great sense of humour and we had many good times together, though I'm ashamed to say that I completely lost touch with him after leaving the army and have no idea what happened to him. He was an actor and he had studied at the Guildhall before going into the army. His name was Peter Bridgemont and he was the son of Leslie Bridgemont, a senior producer in the Variety Department of the BBC with whom I was to work briefly a few years later. Peter's generous help to me with my audition pieces for RADA went far beyond the claims of friendship; he listened to them and recorded them for me so I could hear myself. One was a set piece from Shakespeare; my own choice was a speech from Marlowe's *Dr Faustus* which I had seen performed by Robert Harris at Stratford-on-Avon a year or two previously. Peter certainly did a good job on me, for I passed the audition and got the essential government grant to allow me to stay in London during term time.

Thankfully the blockade of Berlin came to an end almost on cue and demobilisation was resumed. I travelled to a depot in York where I chose a demob suit, a trench coat and a soft felt hat I thought becoming for an actor and returned briefly to Coventry. Then on to London for the audition and so, in a very short space of time, to the Royal Academy of Dramatic Art.

[6]

RADA in 1949 still bore the scars of bomb damage during World War Two. The principal loss had been the theatre in which end of term productions took place and, until the proposed new Vanbrugh Theatre could be built, students had to make do with a much smaller stage and auditorium in the basement of the building in Gower Street.

This post war period had other problems; most of the men were returning from the forces and were therefore two or three years older than most of the girls, who came straight from school. Furthermore, there was still a tendency among some young women to think of RADA as a rather trendy sort of finishing school, so there was inevitably a confrontation between the worldly-wise ex-servicemen and the possibly rather less dedicated debs.

On our first day we were welcomed in the small theatre by the academy secretary, a rather formidable, aquiline-featured, turban-clad lady, Nancy Brown, who alarmed some of us with her opening remark: 'The Royal Academy is a school for stars.'

The principal was an elderly and enfeebled gentleman, Sir Kenneth Barnes, whose two sisters Dame Irene and Violet Vanbrugh had both been distinguished Shakespearean actresses at the turn of the century and, although of advanced years, still gave occasional classes. They both represented the 'grand dame' school of acting which was still to be seen on stage in performances by the likes of Dame Sybil Thorndike and Dame Edith Evans, though it has now completely disappeared from our television-flavoured theatre.

The teaching staff were a rather mixed bag; there were specialists in subjects such as voice training, fencing and dancing, and producers, or directors, as they are called today, who were for the most part either working actors topping up their income or actors who never did any other work scratching a living as best they could.

My two main voice teachers throughout two years as a student were Clifford Turner, who is still regarded by some as the greatest of experts and who is the author of definitive books on the subject, and a former opera singer, Freddie Ranelagh, who was a delightful man, by this time already in his eighties I believe. His classes almost invariably consisted entirely of breath-control exercises and singing and were at the same time both fun and incalculably useful.

The oddest classes of all were conducted by a very camp gentleman named Theodore Constable, who, aided by a bearded, taciturn companion who played piano, guided us weekly through a sequence of movement exercises he claimed to have evolved from ancient friezes and which he based on what he called the 'six basic Greek positions'. The intention was to teach us how to posture and gesture and to know what our arms and legs were doing even if we couldn't see them, but I fear the main things they achieved were much laughing up sleeves and sniggering behind backs.

Theo did accomplish a great deal in teaching us how to relax through a form almost of self-hypnosis; he did attempt to remove inhibitions through freedom of expression in spontaneous movement, but I fear he also confused some minds – certainly mine – by giving us a lecture on theosophy, at the drop of a hat. I didn't understand a word of it then and I can't remember a word of it now.

Other movement classes were in the hands, literally and embarrassingly, of an elderly former ballet dancer, Madame Lydia Sokolova, whose bizarre appearance was not greatly enhanced by a very evident wig and total lack of eyebrows. Her great forte was stylised period movement and her great ploy to pose herself as Juliet and then to place young men in a suitably recumbent posture which entailed much manual adjustment of their groins and crotches.

Each term there would be daily classes in all of the subjects mentioned so far, with perhaps ballet and fencing once or twice a

[53]

week. The rest of each day was spent in rehearsing a play which would be given a couple of performances at the end of term. We would then gather in Sir Kenneth's office for his rather bumbling, useless critique; it was always wisest to accept this without question. Unfortunately that has never been easy for me. I still remember with a modicum of shame sitting in the old gentleman's room after a performance of *Richard III* in which I thought I had done rather well. When it came to my turn Sir Kenneth said, 'Ah, ummmm, Brian, yes. Good, but a rather lightweight performance, I felt. Do you know what I mean?'

'No, Sir Kenneth,' I replied, to everyone else's irritation, for unhappily he didn't know what he meant by it himself and spent several minutes demonstrating the fact.

There were, as we moved towards and into the fifties, several American students at RADA and for one term they included Dolores Gray, who was appearing in London at the time as Annie Oakley in *Annie Get Your Gun*. There was also a handsome young man named Dale Robertson who had already starred in an American television series 'Wells Fargo'. It was pretty obvious that their brief stay in our midst was solely to be able to add to their curriculum vitae back home the magic words, '. . . studied at the Royal Academy of Dramatic Art in London'.

Another American with whom I became quite friendly for a while was very different. He was immensely tall, saturnine in appearance, much older than most of us, and professionally Jewish in a way that only Americans seem to have perfected. On one occasion he was rehearsing *The Shop at Sly Corner*, directed by one of the more *outrée* ladies at the Academy, Mary Duff. She shook her bangle-festooned arms and cried, 'No, Al, no. Try to remember that this man is a shop keeper. Make him more Jewish, much more Jewish. I want to see a lot more Ikey-kikey!'

'Lady,' drawled Al, 'I am Jewish. And my father was a shop keeper.'

Al Hurwitz was this splendid man's name and he claimed to have worked in Hollywood, playing sheriff in several 'B' westerns, which impressed some of us enormously. Sadly, in recent years I have searched a rather extensive personal collection of movie histories without finding any clues to his screen existence, but I still like to think he was telling the truth. He certainly knew a great deal about acting technique and was often of great help to me, watching my performance and noticing difficulties that teachers had failed to spot. Once, I remember, he told me that I looked as though I had left a coat hanger in my jacket, so much tension was there around my shoulders. He then worked with me on relaxing those shoulder muscles. Al Hurwitz was a man who could have made a great contribution to theatre, I feel sure.

One of my closest RADA friends was an actor who uses the stage name of Derek Waring. On one occasion we both stood at the back of the Academy theatre; we were simultaneously smitten by a young actress who was playing a fourteen year old boy! Her name was Dorothy Tutin and a few months later we were both to be members of the Old Vic Company which she joined to play an enchanting Princess Katherine to Alec Clunes' Henry V. Some years later, though, she married Derek Waring and their daughter, Amanda, looking for all the world like her mother all that time ago, has now made a considerable mark herself in the profession.

Another very dear friend was the late Derek Royle who was a marvellous comedian and a truly accomplished acrobat. During our last term at the Academy we shared a flat in Streatham that belonged to Shaw Taylor, now the familiar face of 'Police Five' and the like; in those days he was an unknown actor playing a season at Aberdeen repertory company. During the happy weeks that we shared that flat Derek kept me endlessly entertained with his self-taught sleight of hand, vanishing cigarettes and producing them out of my ear and so on. We also enjoyed a brief trip to a college in Loughborough with a company from RADA performing a play called *And So to Bed* in which Derek gave a magical performance as Samuel Pepys and I played King Charles II.

Some years later, by one of those coincidences which seem more common in the entertainment business than elsewhere, I was the

[55]

compère of a television pop music show called 'Thank Your Lucky Stars'; Jane, the girl who usually made me up, was destined to become Mrs Royle. Even more years later, when I had become the host of the radio programme 'Round Midnight', a beautiful young actress came in for an interview and told me her name was Carol Royle. I remarked that it was a fairly unusual name and asked if she knew my old friend Derek. 'I should think so,' she said. 'He's my Dad.'

The last time I saw Derek was at the newly re-opened Theatre Royal in Bath, when he was appearing in a revival of the John Chapman farce *Simple Spymen* with which Brian Rix had chosen to make his stage return after many years. 'Round Midnight' was broadcast live from the stage and a happy time was had by all, especially since John Chapman was also there – he too had been a contemporary and friend of both of us at RADA.

The news of Derek's death was obviously a shock to those of us who knew him intimately, for he always seemed to have an abundance of life. It is, nevertheless, comforting to remember that our last meeting was over a drink or two in the environment that we both loved best.

Among the actors who directed plays at RADA one that I recall most vividly was Alexander Guage, eventually to be a definitive Friar Tuck in a television Robin Hood series. Suitably rotund in face and figure, he was born to play the part; he had a merry disposition to boot.

When he directed my class in a play, he was appearing nightly in a long-running hit at the Criterion Theatre called *Traveller's Joy*. It had already been on for a couple of years, and at the end of our afternoon rehearsals he would always adjourn with a few of us to the nearest pub and, as if it were a ritual, he would swiftly down a couple of pints with whisky chasers. At the time I prudishly thought it was a dreadful thing to do before a performance, not realising that he needed some sort of boost to go on with a fairly mediocre play night after night. His need became clearer to me a couple of years later when *Traveller's Joy* became one of the first plays in which I myself appeared in rep. Fortunately for me and for the production the wages at that time were so low that the price of even a single pint was beyond my meagre means.

One of the biggest problems for students in the middle of the century, as I have no doubt is still the case today, was in finding suitable accommodation at an affordable price. My first digs had been located for me by a friend of my father and were with a congenial family in Edgware; meals were taken with their two sons and another lodger who was a law student. The main problem was that one was at the mercy of the Northern Line tube for getting home at night; that soon began to interfere with social life lived at what might be termed 'theatrical' hours.

This was forcibly impressed on me after a wild night out with another American, Michael Lewis, the son of the famous novelist, Sinclair Lewis, author of *Babbit* and *Dodsworth* among other stories, not much read nowadays, perhaps, but immensely popular at that time.

Michael was only eighteen when he came to RADA, but was well over six feet tall. He was more than adequately financially stable compared with most of us, and was used to a pretty sophisticated life-style. When he learned that I was unacquainted with cocktails he made it his mission to introduce me to the Old Fashioned. The first few bars we visited were as ignorant of the mixture as I was but we finally got lucky in Scott's Cocktail Bar near Leicester Square; the evening degenerated into a pub crawl. Refreshed by humbler brews we finally fetched up in the Blue Posts near Tottenham Court Road, where we were picked up by a couple of rather downmarket ladies of the night. Packed into a cab with these companions, Michael and I both had sufficient remnants of good sense in our addled brains to bail out on the far side of the taxi and to run off into the night, pursued by anguished cries of abuse which turned the air more blue than the posts in the name of the pub we had just left.

I did manage to get back to Edgware that night, though I had no recollection of the journey, and despite a gently amused reception

[57]

from my host the following morning, I felt the time had come for a move.

My next abode was a one-room flatlet in Holland Park, close to the famous Portobello Road street market. I was introduced to this by another fellow student, Ibrahim Alkazi, known to us as Elk, who is I believe now a distinguished actor or drama teacher in his native Bombay. He was the only married member of our class and his wife had accompanied him to London. They were both extremely kind to me and introduced me to really excellent Indian cooking.

Sadly, domestic economy has never been one of my strong points and it has been my great good fortune to have that side of life looked after by my wife, but in student days it grew harder and harder to balance the books so that even a one-room apartment became an onerous responsibility, and the offer of a loaned flat, shared as I have said with Derek Royle, was a godsend during my final term.

I was invariably broke long before any term ended, but was always able to retreat to the haven of my home in Coventry during vacations where nothing was ever expected for my keep and a room was always kept ready for me. This was the room that had been occupied by my dear old Gran who had died at the great age of ninety-four while I was with the army in Germany. On the very day I returned on demob leave my mother took me to see the room, which had been redecorated, and told me that it was now mine for as long as I wanted. On the way back downstairs I heard, quite distinctly, a dry sort of cough or clearing of the throat which was a habit of Gran's, emanating from the room we had just left. When I told my mother this she surprised me by saying that she had had the same experience herself shortly after Gran's death. We neither of us ever heard it again and most likely it was a sound in my mind's ear much as it is now as I write these words, but it was a strange moment.

Although it was one thing to accept the generous hospitality of my far from wealthy parents during shorter holidays, the long summer vacation loomed as a real problem, until my father had the inspired idea of asking a farmer friend if he would provide me with bed, board and modest pocket money in return for harvest time labour. Happily he agreed.

[7]

It was only due to one of life's minor miracles that I was able to get to George Barrett's farm in Thorpe Mandeville at all during my first long vacation. That term I was more hard up than ever; completely broke, without even a penny in my pocket. I remember standing outside the Dominion Theatre in Tottenham Court Road paralysed with despair; I hadn't a clue as to how to get out of my predicament. Then, from the thousands of passers-by, a girl I knew faintly from the Academy appeared and asked me what I was doing there. When I told her, she said that she could lend me ten shillings till the start of next term if I liked, and it was thanks to this unlikely occurrence that I managed to get home.

That kind girl's face, though alas not her name, is firmly imprinted in my memory, for she was also a person of great courage. More mature than most of the young ladies in my class she had gone to university before RADA but then had suffered a stroke which left one side of her face partially paralysed. By dint of far above average application to our voice exercises she had managed to improve her speech enormously, though whether she ever managed to obtain employment in the theatre I don't know.

The journey from Coventry to the farm was easy and cost free, since in those days I still kept a bicycle at home and a matter of forty miles or so was nothing out of the ordinary.

As I look from my window today, at my home in Kent, surrounded as it is by farmland, I am forcibly reminded of the extent to which agriculture has changed in this second half of the twentieth century. The farming that I knew in Oxfordshire must have changed but little in a hundred years, save for the replacement of the working horse by the tractor. We still cut the corn with an aged binder, built the stooks into stacks of some ten or a dozen, then collected them on carts to construct ricks which were then thatched to protect them from the elements.

Later in the summer a rented threshing box would arrive with a large group of casual workers; the previous year's ricks would be dismantled and the stooks fed into the top of the box. This was a hot, noisy and uncomfortable job, for the threshed corn poured out of one aperture to be gathered in sacks, and the chaff was accumulated on a groundsheet that was gathered up periodically and removed; a proportion of it inevitably found its way into one's clothing where it caused itching almost beyond endurance.

One other aspect of a day's threshing was regarded by real country folk as a kind of sport, but as I have always been shamefully squeamish about rodents it was one that I didn't want to know about. Almost invariably a rick would have provided winter quarters for rats and as it diminished under the thresher these poor terrified creatures would run screaming and squealing, falling prey to men and boys with dogs and sticks.

I am glad to have had the experience at first hand of this nineteenth-century way of life, for it was already beginning to change. A couple of years later my farmer friend bought his first combine harvester and the whole harvest process was telescoped into one operation; cutting, threshing and bailing all took place simultaneously. Doubtless this has been an improvement in terms of productivity, but as a way of life I'm not so sure. It was with a wave of wistful nostalgia that just a year ago I watched a Greek farmer on Zante peacefully scything a small field of corn while his tethered donkey champed contentedly on the straw in a corner.

But perhaps I should explain how this rustic bliss came the way of an industrial city dweller.

My parents had introduced me at about the age of five to the Wilde family, who lived at the time in a cottage in the village of Cropredy, just a few miles outside Banbury. How they met in the first place I cared not at the time and strangely never chose to ask in later years, as I felt there was some connection with my father's first wife and she was never mentioned.

Mrs Wilde was one of the kindest, gentlest people it has ever been my privilege to meet. Her voice would have delighted Shakespeare, for it was soft, gentle and low, and come to think of it her accent would most likely have been familiar to him as well. She had five children, all of whom I was to come to know well over the ensuing years.

The eldest was Joan, who trained as a teacher. She was engaged when I first met her – to a pilot who was, in the early thirties, a member of a very small and select band. With the advent of war he went straight into the Air Force but was regrettably shot down over enemy territory where he was imprisoned for the duration. His mother, for reasons of her own, wrote him malicious letters about Joan; as a result of these he broke off their engagement, to her great distress.

George Barrett knew the Wilde family and began to court Joan. He told her that he knew she loved her former fiancé, but if she would marry him he would do his utmost to make her a good husband. Happily Joan accepted him and he was every bit as good as his word. His father had been a farmer himself and had set up all his sons with places of their own, wisely requiring George to share a farm with his brother Ralph who was, as country folk used to say, 'strong i' th'arm but weak i' th' head'.

Joan's oldest brother Ivor was something of an oddity who had acquired numerous specialised skills such as thatching but never seemed content with the farming life. Indeed he did at one time stand unsuccessfully as a Labour candidate for Parliament.

The middle member of the Wilde family was Maureen, whom I knew least of all until much later. She had married, less than wisely, a man who was known to suffer from burning jealousy and I think there was often much unhappiness. I hope things got better for her.

Then there was Brian, who was only a year or two older than myself. He joined the Palestine Police when he was eighteen years old and died in circumstances never properly explained.

[62]

The youngest child was Dulcie who I think truly loved me when we were about six. She lost an eye as a result of an accident with an airgun and then became a nurse in Oxford. She eventually married an Italian she had met while he was a prisoner of war in England, and went to Italy to make his pasta and bear his children.

The father of the family, Dick Wilde, was a Lancastrian who never lost his native accent despite all his years living in the midst of the Oxfordshire and Warwickshire farming communities. He was a gardener by trade and worked for one or another of the large houses in the area, usually the home of a Major this or a Colonel that, and as a tied cottage often went with the job the Wilde family tended to move from village to village every few years; the final move was to Thorpe Mandeville, which was the village closest to George's first farm.

When I lived and worked on this farm we had no electricity; we used oil lamps and candles about the home. Nor was there any running water; our daily needs were obtained from a pump over a well close to the kitchen door. The working days were long indeed, with George rising at the crack of dawn to milk his cows and feed his pigs and then leading his work force – his brother, one labourer and me – in the fields. I learned to drive, but never very satisfactorily to start, the tractors and it usually fell to my lot to tow the binder, which was operated by brother Ralph. This was an ancient piece of equipment which used to break down about once for every circuit of the field, when I would be halted by a bull-like roar of 'Whoooooaaa!' from Ralph, who always managed to imply that it was somehow my fault, and would sulkily set about mending the 'damn fing' with much grumbling and cursing.

Another regular chore for me was to stand on a trailer with a pitch fork, laying the stooks of corn as they were thrown to me by other men working in the fields. The higher this pile grew the more difficult and the more dangerous the job became. On one occasion there was also another unlooked-for hazard. Maureen's husband had for some unaccountable reason, and totally without justification, got it into his head that I was after his wife. He managed with

[63]

great accuracy to toss stooks which often carried nettles and thistles in them so that they landed unerringly in the middle of my back, leaving me looking as though I had been flogged at the mast.

In spite of long hours of quite hard work our modest leisure time was often spent surprisingly energetically. George was a very good tennis player and had got permission to use the private court of the local manor house; the owners were the landlords of his two hundred acres. Sadly I was always a rabbit at tennis which was particularly unfortunate on these occasions as we were usually joined by two attractive young women from the 'big house' who understandably made no bones about who they wanted as a partner.

Our other main sporting activity was snooker, played on a three-quarter size table in George's front parlour. The room was big enough for the table, but without much space to spare which led to some strangely acrobatic shots. George was damn good at this too, curse it.

Two summers passed pleasantly in this way and the next time I visited the farm it was to spend my honeymoon there, but that belongs to another part of the story. George eventually bought another farm, with a beautiful Georgian house, in the village of Gawcott in Buckinghamshire and for a while commuted between the two. Joan sadly died several years ago and Maureen has become George's companion in his retirement.

Although this rural interlude may sit strangely in the life story of someone who has spent almost all his working days in the entertainment business, it was nevertheless of great importance to me and certainly left me with many treasured memories.

[8]

My second year at RADA, 1950, was an immensely enjoyable experience for the most part, just slightly tinged with anxiety as I became increasingly aware of harsh reality looming at the end of it. It was difficult then and is difficult now for a youngster at the end of training to get an agent and a job; without a strong degree of resilience in one's nature despair can soon become a familiar companion.

All of that, however, still seemed a long way off when there were such delights as the Roehampton Theatrical Garden Party to experience. This was an all-star wing-ding, with familiar faces doing much of the work, running stalls ('Oh, look! There's Mary Morris') and generally fund-raising. On the only occasion I visited this event with a small group of contemporaries we were lucky that one of our number had been appointed barman, alongside the extremely camp Douglas Byng. Drinks flowed across to us endlessly, free of charge, while Dougie kept up a waspish but very amusing commentary. Many years later I interviewed him on a couple of programmes and, despite his great age, for he was then in his nineties, his personality had changed but little. One of his favourite stories against himself was of how, during a Charlot revue, he minced across the stage, all in black, blissfully unaware that his tights had split at the front displaying, as he put it, his all 'like a red carnation'.

Then there was a totally astonishing RADA Ball held at the Lyceum Theatre as a fund raiser for the new Vanbrugh Theatre at the Academy. The volunteer cabaret was one that money could not have bought. Richard Attenborough was the master of ceremonies, introducing Vanessa Lee, accompanied at the piano by Ivor

Novello; there was a fourteen year old Julie Andrews, who in those days was the surprise element in a variety act by Ted and Barbara Andrews, and the top of the bill was Paul Robson. I remember now the feelings of a totally unknown twenty-one year old, sitting on the floor watching these household names with an awareness of somehow being a part of it all.

By this time there was a growing realisation for most of us that classes were all very well and necessary, but the performance was the thing. In addition to the official productions there was a great wish and willingness to mount student produced shows and for one of these, a revue, a member of the cast was Alfred Hitchcock's daughter. She had been on holiday in New York and seen *South Pacific* which had not yet arrived in London; she directed some of us in numbers from that show. I was one of the marines in the rumbustious chorus 'Nothing Like a Dame' and she herself gave an enthusiastic rendition of 'Gonna Wash That Man Right out of my Hair'. It was fun to have been part of this unauthorised London première.

In the public performance offered as a show case for students, to which agents and managers were invited, it was the practice to share the major roles, which was obviously fair if a little confusing; imagine watching a *Richard III* in which the main protagonist changed from an American to English to Indian in the course of an afternoon.

When the time came for our all important end of course public show we were horrified to learn that it was to be a dreadful old melodrama called *Secrets*. This was by Rudolph Besier whose one great success was *The Barretts of Wimpole Street* which was produced at the Queen's in 1930 and ran for two years with Gwen Ffrangcon-Davies as Elizabeth Moulton-Barrett. Besier, however, was born in 1878 and his much earlier *Secrets* reflected the theatre of his youth. The hero was the son of an aristocratic family somehow disgraced in the first act, so that he and his young wife emigrate in the second act to make their fortune in the Wild West. Their log cabin is attacked by cattle thieves, the brave little woman

[66]

is shot and dies in his arms, and then in act three he returns a sadder, wiser but richer man.

To my total consternation I drew the middle act, in which I had to blaze away with six-guns through a small window in the cabin. In our tiny theatre the back wall was not far from the upstage setting line, and for this play some black velvet drapes covered the cyclorama. As an economy I was not allowed to have blank cartridges in my guns until the actual performance, so no one had realised that even a blank spits out glowing pieces of cordite. We soon found out because while my performance may not have set the town alight, it played havoc with the black curtains, peppering them with smoking holes.

It was at this performance that I became one of the six students chosen for employment by Hugh Hunt and it has always been a point of pride for me that there must be singularly few actors who have been selected to play in Shakespeare at the Vic on the strength of their prowess as a cowboy.

Oddly enough my experience with the blazing revolvers was to be reflected in an unfortunate accident at the Old Vic. The second play in which I appeared was *Captain Brassbound's Conversion* by Shaw with Roger Livesey as Brassbound and his wife Ursula Jeans as Lady Cicely. I doubled as an Arab and an American sailor. As the Arab I was required, with several others, to cavort about firing a rifle, again with blanks of course. Unfortunately the very fine actor James Grout had to wave his arms about in semblance of panic in the midst of this mêlée, and managed to flap one of his hands across the muzzle of my gun at the moment of firing. His palm was peppered with small particles of cordite which had to be removed extremely painfully during a visit to hospital. He has forgiven me and indeed we have remained friends ever since.

Although the Arabs in the play were not given lines by Shaw, we were tutored by a gentleman from the Egyptian embassy to utter, in Arabic, such phrases as 'There is an American gunboat in the harbour,' which we shouted while leaping about firing our guns. But one of our group, Laurence Davidson, had spent his military

[67]

service in Cairo and learned a smattering of Arabic; he tutored us in some quite different phrases so that in some performances at least we leapt about screaming very naughty things which decency forbids me to repeat here in English.

My recent return to theatre has shown me that some things change but little and that many actors, especially young ones, still indulge in attempts to make each other laugh, or 'corpse' as it's called. It is perhaps a little childish and irresponsible but I find it understandable after a run of several weeks, especially among those playing minor parts.

Mind you, some quite senior members of the profession have been known to indulge in such misdemeanours from time to time. I have even heard that the distinguished Paul Schofield is a past master at making his fellow actors laugh, though I am unable to speak from personal experience in that case. However, Roger Livesey was a great practical joker and would often set up quite complicated ploys that had a habit of backfiring on him by failing to work and making him laugh himself.

In the 1951 season, Roger played Sir Toby Belch and Robert Eddison was Sir Andrew Aguecheek in *Twelfth Night*; Roger was a great joker and Robert had something of a reputation for being a giggler. Towards the end of the play Aguecheek enters with a 'bloody coxcomb' given him by Sebastian and he's followed by Sir Toby, drunk. In this production they had some business in which Robert had to pull off one of Roger's boots. Roger had rigged up a device with a battery in his pocket and a wire down his tights to a little red bulb on his toe. The plan was to make it light up when the boot was removed, thereby reducing Robert to a quivering wreck. The device failed of course, Robert saw nothing of it and Roger was reduced to fits of giggles himself. He then explained to the audience in his curtain speech what should have happened.

During the course of this season there was a plan to take the company to Australia at the end of the year and then to return for the following season at the Vic. I was summoned by Hugh Hunt and told that I was considered to be one of the more promising of

[68]

the junior members of the company, and that they wanted to build me up gradually with more important roles. I couldn't believe my luck. Then came the blow that I was to discover was typical of this profession. Suddenly Hugh Hunt was dispossessed and it was announced that Tyrone Guthrie was taking over as director and would audition the entire company. By this time I had become engaged to Pamela Wickington and we chose to do a joint audition with a scene from *The Taming of the Shrew*. Alas, the great Guthrie did not share Hunt's view of my promise and we were not invited to stay on with the company after all.

The season came to an end with a week of performances of *Henry V* in Liverpool. On the last night Roger Livesey delivered an outrageous but very funny curtain speech in which he told the audience that many of us had hoped to be returning for another season but that plans had changed. 'Instead', he bellowed, 'you're going to get Donald Wolfit, so the best of luck to you all.'

This all happened in July 1951 and Pamela and I planned to marry in August at a church on Goose Green in East Dulwich, close to her parents' home. We had invited members of the Old Vic company, many of whom attended.

My best man was Johnny Walker, who had been one of my friends at RADA and another of the recruits to the Old Vic. He shared a South Kensington flat with a couple of his gay acquaintances and it was in this unlikely apartment that I spent my last night of bachelordom. The wedding was to be a full dress affair, but to save expense Johnny and I, immaculately attired in Moss Bros. best with grey toppers and all, travelled to East Dulwich on the top deck of a Number Twelve bus!

I don't know whether many grooms remember much of their wedding ceremonies. I certainly have little recollection of mine, though Pamela always swears that when kneeling at the altar I kept on sinking lower and lower. After the reception we left for our honeymoon at my friends George and Joan's farm in Thorpe Mandeville and there spent an idyllic three weeks, our evenings romantically illuminated by oil lamps.

[69]

We returned to London and a small flat on the top storey of my in-laws' house to start out married life as impecunious, out of work, actors. The lack of funds was to continue for several years but happily the unemployment problem was soon to be resolved.

[9]

Like many actors, then and now, we had firmly decided there was no way we would even try to manage to exist on the dole if we could find temporary work whilst waiting for interviews and auditions. It was fairly easy for Pamela as she had wisely trained as a shorthand-typist before going to drama school, but I had no skills and had to settle for brain-numbing jobs as a clerk.

Quite the worst example of this demeaning occupation came with a spell in the large clerical pool of a well-known paint firm. I was required to extrapolate figures from invoices and transfer them to a filing card index which in theory provided a sort of running stock check. It was totally undemanding and the work dished out first thing in the morning could easily be dealt with before lunch. I was, however, told quite firmly to slow down before everyone else was expected to work at the same pace. There was little option but to comply as I had no intention of staying for any longer than absolutely necessary. What an indictment of a ridiculous system.

Eventually we found an advertisement in the columns of the *Stage* concerning vacancies in the 'Mime Theatre Company' of which we had never heard but which was to furnish us with about three months' work and dining-out stories for the rest of our lives.

The company had been founded a few years earlier on his demobilisation by the then completely unknown Clifford Williams, now, of course, a very well known West End director and also an associate director of the Royal Shakespeare Company. He had assembled a group of some eight or ten actors who, with their joint funds, purchased a second-hand pantechnicon in which they planned to travel around the country with their props and costumes giving fit-up performances of Clifford's devising wherever they could find audiences. It was one of those worthy schemes that are too wide of reality to endure successfully.

By the time we presented ourselves for interview the Mime Theatre Company had dwindled to four and occasionally five in number and the pantechnicon was long gone. Clifford Williams, or Willie as he has been known to me for almost forty years now, led from the front, devising, directing and performing as well as arranging all the bookings. I don't think he had been inundated with applications for the vacancies and so we were readily accepted at the sum of five pounds each a week. Transport, we were assured, would be paid for but we should have to find and pay for our nightly accommodation out of our pittance. Remarkably, as it turned out, it was still possible to do this in late 1951 and we were also able to save a pound a week for our rent in London.

The structure of the programme was a lecture on the history of theatre delivered by Willie, followed by the mime version of the players' scene from *Hamlet* (Willie was the King, Pamela was the Queen and I was the murderer) and then, adding words to movement, we performed a one act play which was usually *The Bear* by Chekhov and sometimes a farce by O'Casey, the title of which I have completely forgotten. There were other occasional variations, as you shall discover.

Rehearsals were conducted in a bleak church hall in Hackney close to the house where Willie lived with his parents. I think he had done some sort of deal with the vicar to have the use of the premises rent-free in return for a free performance for that worthy's boys' club members before we set off on the road. A potentially dangerous situation as it turned out, as many of these members also belonged to a tough gang, the Hoxton Lads, who were alleged to have dismembered a detective inspector prior to posting the pieces down a drain. Their main purpose in attending the boys' club was to gain access to the snooker table there and it was hard to imagine them being particularly fascinated by classical mime and Chekhov.

The day of this 'preview' dawned and indeed passed without any untoward incident so far as we could tell. At least until afterwards. Then we discovered that the dear boys had first locked us into our dressing room, the vestry, and then pocketed the full set of snooker balls as lethal missiles should our performance fail to please. Fortunately a white faced curate discovered both the balls' loss and their whereabouts in the nick of time, thereby saving our limbs if not our lives.

The first official performance was at a rather posh girls' school which had an assembly hall the like of which I have never seen elsewhere before or since. The stage was built across one corner and was therefore triangular in shape which was no particular problem in itself, but the audience was seated square on to the end of the hall so that they were obliged to watch us glancing, as it were, over their right shoulders. We were playing in daylight during the afternoon as was to prove the general rule, so we could see the girls as clearly as they could see us, but this strange seating arrangement made them appear for all the world as though they were gathered together for some other purpose entirely and that we were distracting their attention by doing strange things in the corner.

Adaptability was obviously going to be the watchword for the next few months. We arrived at the second venue, in Devonshire, to find we were expected to perform in the school's very large open air theatre which had an acting area of about half an acre. Our mimes had been meticulously choreographed to gramophone records with movements timed to fit specific bars of music. On the previous day's triangular stage this had presented no problem, but in this vast open air space we had to break cover from behind box hedges and then gallop about like mad things to cover the ground and keep time with the music.

The next morning, on the train to Penzance, Willie broke the news that the company had visited this day's school during the previous tour and we should need therefore to improvise a different programme. His master plan was that he would extend his own introductory lecture and the other three of us should raid the costume boxes and come on as he called us to demonstrate period movement. Amazingly, all went smoothly and well until we were taken to the headmistress's study for tea, sandwiches and conversation at the end of our show. After congratulating us warmly the dear lady asked us how long we had been doing this sort of work. 'Oh, we've only just st . . .' my honest wife began to reply until brought to a halt by a swift kick under the table from Willie. 'And do tell me,' continued the headmistress, who clearly saw this as a golden opportunity to learn the tricks of the trade, 'how were you able to find out the position of the legs during a curtsy, or in the court dances?' 'Oh,' said Willie without batting an eyelid, 'there are books, you know. With illustrations. With diaphanous skirts.'

There is no answer to that, as an old friend of mine always used to say when confronted with a monumental bluff.

The usual daily routine on arrival in a new town was for Pamela and the other girl in the company to set off in search of digs for the night with strict instructions not to take anything that was more than seven shillings and sixpence (less than forty pence today) for bed and breakfast, while Willie and I set up our props and borrowed anything that was going in the way of screens and lights. He had also decreed before the tour that we must always accept any hospitality offered, be it food or lodging, and if we ever arrived in a place where any of us had friends who might offer free accommodation, we must pay a share of the costs of the others. He'd really got this shoe-string operation down to a fine art.

Locating digs at or below the suggested maximum was, surprisingly, easier than one might have imagined, although first appearances could often be deceptive. I recall arriving in a bleak northern town one bitterly cold day and tramping the dingy streets for some time without finding anything. Then we came upon a boarding house through the window of which we could see a coal fire giving a cosy glow to the room. We decided to accept whatever was offered before the front door had been opened. Alas, it turned out to be one of the worst places we ever found and the only time in our sheltered young lives that we met up with bed bugs. The food was uneatable as well. We couldn't get away early enough the next morning.

As a counter to that I must mention a delightful house we had the good fortune to find when visiting Wrexham, on the Welsh border. This was a boarding house mostly frequented by travelling salesmen and it was run by a dear old lady, severely cross-eyed. Our room was clean and comfortable and the food was good. One afternoon, when the salesmen were out selling, Pamela and I were invited to tea in the good lady's parlour and then asked rather coyly if we would like to see her hats. Not feeling that a refusal was in order we said we should love to, and spent the next half hour biting our tongues, digging our finger nails into our palms, and trying anything else that might prevent us from laughing, as we were treated to one of the most bizarre fashion shows ever. From bag after bag our landlady produced countless confections, each more hideous than its predecessor, and, staring at us with her pronounced squint, asked if we didn't find it lovely. Pamela, I have to say, deserved an Oscar for her convincing display of enthusiasm.

An embarrassing instance for all parties concerned was on one of the dates at an arts club. A distinguished member of this club, the wife of a celebrated QC as it transpired, had offered in advance to provide hospitality for all four of us. We think she must have been expecting Laurence Olivier and Vivien Leigh at the very least. After the performance she drove us to a breathtaking mansion some miles away, then, after showing us to our beautiful rooms, left us alone to a cold collation in the kitchen. Obviously too polite to go back on her arrangement, she was clearly going to spend no more time in our scruffy presence than she could help.

Even worse was to come. Early the next morning her pampered offspring crashed into our bedroom screaming blue murder and yelling for these horrid intruders to be sent packing. A business-like nanny eventually bustled them out and away and a little later, after one must admit a sumptuous breakfast, we were bustled away pretty smartly ourselves.

For the most part our performances seemed to be enjoyable and especially in schools the audiences were as enthusiastic and

[75]

involved as you might find anywhere. In *The Bear* a landowner visits a young widow to collect a debt incurred by her late husband. She can't pay on the spot and he refuses to leave until she does. He gets into a frightful rage and yells and shouts at her while, predictably, becoming attracted to her. Finally he suggests a duel and she provides a pair of pistols. By this time, it would have become clear to an adult audience that nobody is going to shoot anybody, but we still remember with relish a small boy sitting in the front row at one performance completely absorbed in the action. As Pamela stood before me, irresolutely waving her pistol in the air, he shouted, 'Go on, shoot him you silly cow!'

Spontaneous participation was, of course, one thing, but owing to our slight resources and minimal manpower we were frequently obliged to rely on conscripted participation, occasionally with disastrous results. At a girls' school in Folkestone for one of our rare evening performances in a hall with no stage, we had included a 'Harlequinade' in the programme, at the end of which we needed a blackout to get off unseen. The only way of achieving this was for someone in an adjacent corridor, with no view of the acting area, to throw a mains switch and then after a suitable interval to throw it back again. A senior prefect was chosen as a truly responsible assistant and told that the end of a particular piece of music was the cue for the blackout. She should then count slowly to ten and put the lights on once more.

Whether this onerous chore proved too much for the dear girl, whether even this activity induced an attack of nerves or whether, perish the thought, she harboured a strong streak of malice it's hard to tell. Be that as it may, the blackout duly came on cue, then after the quickest count to ten imaginable the lights came on to reveal four sheepish actors creeping towards a door carrying their stools.

It was, alas, equally possible for members of the cast to create even worse havoc. Willie once regaled me with a story about my predecessor who had also played the murderer in the *Hamlet* mime sequence. Part of this role involved making an exit to bring down the curtain for the 'dead' king to leave the stage unobserved by the

[76]

audience. The murderer on this occasion was rather short-sighted and, deprived of his glasses, failed to see the gap between the side of the stage and the side wall of the hall. He made his exit all right, then fell off the edge and, striking his head on a radiator, was knocked completely unconscious, leaving Willie recumbent and stranded centre stage.

After a few hoarsely whispered imprecations to 'pull the bloody curtain' the king was suddenly miraculously restored to life. Rising to his feet, Willie addressed the audience, saying, 'Of course in the Elizabethan theatre there was no curtain so that dead bodies had to get up and walk off, as I am going to do now.' For sensitive and curious souls I should perhaps add that the poor murderer soon recovered consciousness and showed no signs of lasting damage.

Far and away my own worst experience with the Mime Theatre Company occurred away from stage and performance when we were visiting a teachers' training college in Warrington. We had been given the use of the art room for changing; this looked out on to a much frequented courtyard. Along the window sill there was a number of clay figures in various stages of completion while the window itself could be covered by a venetian blind. Prior to changing I brought the blind down with a rush, promptly decapitating most of the figures beyond repair. Initially it was mutually agreed that we should keep quiet about the accident, but as we were leaving Willie had second thoughts. He might want to return the following year, he said, and would be grateful if I would go and make a full confession to the principal.

This aspect of return visits must have been a constant source of worry to our leader, but he never seemed to be completely at a loss. His worst fault was that he rarely took the rest of us into his confidence until the last possible moment; this had happened in Cornwall on our third day. Later, in North Wales, he pulled an even more hair-raising stroke. He announced one morning over breakfast that he and I were to take an early bus to the next venue to set things up but as it was a booking where dormitory

[77]

accommodation was to be provided the girls could, as a special treat, come on later.

On that earlier bus Willie then informed me that not only was this a quick return booking, but he had by now used up all his standard lecture material. He had therefore offered as a special extra a morning lecture on speech and movement. He would take care of the movement, he informed me, and I could busk a talk on voice production on the strength of my RADA training.

There was precious little time to get into a state about this as the bus journey was a short one and soon after arrival we were on. It was a salutary exercise in improvisation for me and, I am pleased to be able to add, a tremendous success. Willie was instantly fired with ambition for us to repeat this extra little earner at other venues but since none of such bonuses were likely to find their way into my pocket I was glad that the situation never arose again. Nevertheless I am convinced that the experience set me up for the many times in later years in radio when I have been required to fill in with a lengthy and unforeseen ad lib.

As the year drew to a close and with it our one night stand tour Willie offered to retain Pamela and me after the Christmas break but by this time we had both had enough. Unforgettable though the experience has proved over the years it was pretty hard going at the time. My favourite memory is of a performance in a packed hall at a boys' club in Bradford. For some reason I had to be front of house for the last part of the performance which was an appearance by Willie in his favourite role of Pierrot. Spurned by Columbine and alone on the stage, tears rolling down his white face, he clutched a red rose to his bosom and made a long, heart-broken exit stage left. Accompanied by an equally heartfelt cry from a solitary member of the audience, 'Eeeh, yer gormless bugger!'

[10]

1952 was to prove to be the year in which the first part of the palm-reading actor's prediction for my future came to pass. But at its beginning, with some slight misgivings that perhaps we should have accepted Clifford Williams' invitation to stay another term with his Mime Theatre Company, we were once again out-of-work actors depending on temporary jobs for our existence.

On a visit to my parents' home in Coventry we applied for interviews with Anthony John who was the director of the fairly prestigious Midland Arts Company. Their home base was Coventry, where they played in the theatre of the Technical College, and then took productions for a further run in, I think, Wolverhampton. This meant that each production had a life of several weeks at a period when this was by no means the norm for repertory companies; consequently it was possible to attract actors of a very high standard. To our faint dismay we heard nothing for a long time after our interviews and returned to London and to boring office jobs.

Then we spotted another ad in the *Stage*, this time for two juvenile leads in a company about to play a summer seaside season divided between two resorts. We applied for and were given auditions and were delighted to be offered the jobs, which we accepted. Despite our inexperience it was pretty clear to us that this engagement fell into the dreaded category of 'tatty rep' and would do little to enhance our careers, though I have always believed that one can only gain stature as an actor by acting as opposed to sitting and thinking about it.

While the ink was still wet on our contracts there occurred one of those crossroads in life that leave you forever wondering whether you took the right turning. The Midland Arts Company finally wrote to tell us that they could offer us a joint engagement as assistant stage managers to play as cast. This would have been for a longer period than the jobs we had already accepted and with a company of an unquestionably far higher standard. Pamela was all for cancelling our agreement and taking this new offer, but I refused. I felt that if you took an engagement when you needed it then you were under some sort of moral obligation to go through with it even if a better opportunity presented itself. Not that we would have considered for a moment actually breaking a contract, of course. When our new employers found out what we had done they told us that we had been foolish; we should have asked to be released. They pointed out that we had passed up a good opening while they would have had no trouble in replacing us.

The company we were to work for was called Triumph Productions and had nothing to do with the West End production company of that name today, of course. It had been formed by a married couple whose professional names were Brian Cullis and Alicia Gatrall. They had been working for some years in repertory companies, Alicia especially with theatres run by the famous Harry Hanson, and had decided that they wanted to try running things their own way. They had a staunch fan in an elderly school teacher who was prepared to come in with them as a backer, gambling her savings, and happily in that first season they did actually make a profit.

There were seven acting members in all; Brian directed and he and Alicia played all the leads, while Pamela and I played the juveniles and occasional character parts. Then there was another man engaged solely for character roles and two young girls who were taken on as stage managers, to play if needed. A set of flats had been either bought second hand or hired, and we built and painted our own sets each week. The plan was to play the first eight weeks of the season at the small town of Seaford in Sussex where there was no theatre – performances were given in a church hall – then we moved on to Swanage. There was a small theatre, the Mowlem, on the sea front, but this was occupied by a variety show typical of the period, while we were in another church hall at the back of the town repeating the plays we had already performed in Seaford.

Once the first play had opened the pattern was to rehearse every morning; the afternoon was free for learning lines, then we would perform at night, six nights a week, with matinees if it was wet. We played from Thursday to Wednesday, thus giving holiday makers the chance to see two plays in any one week.

I believe I'm right in saying that in 1952 such requirements were not an infringement of Equity rules, but in any case nobody complained and I think now of that period of our lives with nothing but pleasure.

Fortunately for me learning lines was not a problem at that stage of my life as I had more or less a photographic memory. By the time we had spent a morning rehearsing an act of the play I knew it reasonably well without having to read it over and over again. That facility has long since gone, alas, and it now takes me a good deal longer to absorb words. However, this is not necessarily a drawback as the parrot fashion learning demanded by weekly rep went hand in hand with necessarily superficial performances.

For the first part of our stay in Seaford we were lucky to find excellent digs quite close to the front in a house owned by a lady who was a cook at one of the larger hotels. We catered for ourselves for the most part; some foods, such as cheese and butter, were still rationed but our landlady was extremely generous and was able to supplement our diet from time to time with food from the hotel. One night there was a spectacular thunderstorm with lightning I've only once seen equalled in the South of France – sleep was impossible. The landlady kindly brought us tea and biscuits to our room so that we could enjoy the show.

The plays included in the season were all chosen from lists of past West End successes of recent vintage with the one exception of an old melodrama called *The Chinese Bungalow* which had been a popular vehicle in its day for Matheson Lang. I think that was

[81]

included because Brian Cullis fancied himself as the sinister Chinese Mandarin, Yuan Sing. We also had to borrow a Siamese cat for that play and managed to get hold of one with the inappropriate name of Tweetie Pie.

Alicia's experience with the Harry Hanson company had given her a good grounding in commercial repertory theatre so that everything was done with an eye to box office. This was no opportunity for self-indulgence or experimental theatre and by and large the formula worked. Indeed it was so successful in Swanage that the season had to be extended by a further two weeks.

I have few memories of the plays themselves, though we smile when we recall one particular performance of a comedy called *A Guardsman's Cup of Tea*. I played a Guards Officer and Pamela, his girl friend who lived in a Grace and Favour house. The openings of the first and third acts were similar. In act one the officer arrives at her front door to invite her to a party, and in act three he arrives to be asked 'How was the party?' On this occasion as the curtain first went up, Pamela opened the door to me and asked, 'How was the party?' She claims the look of bewilderment on my face was almost worth it. However, my experiences with Clifford Williams came to my aid because I said, after only the shortest of pauses, 'Oh, that was all right, but I've come to ask you to another one.'

We had only to play one 'matinee if wet' and this one took me somewhat by surprise. Half the holiday makers in Swanage, it seemed, had decided to come and we had to try to squeeze in extra seats at the last minute. This meant a delay in taking up the curtain and that in turn prompted those already inside to start a slow handclap. Not an encouraging experience. However, the play was a very funny one and we won them over in the first few minutes.

The closest we came to a mini disaster occurred when as Pamela was about to make an entrance a huge hairy spider dropped with a plop from her costume to the dressing room floor. She didn't miss her entrance but she did dry on her first line. On returning to the dressing room she tried to persuade the character man to help find the intruder and remove it, but it transpired that he disliked spiders as much as she did and he refused even to look for it.

When the season ended we were again asked if we would like to do another one for the same management; they already had a venue earmarked for the following year. We would have been happy to continue had we not in the meantime come to yet another of life's crossroads and taken a turning which was largely to determine my career for the next forty years.

[11]

Back in London by October 1952 I made one more half-hearted attempt to find another job, other than acting, that I could tolerate. At that time there were regular advertisements in the press for salesmen to be trained to sell encyclopaedias for very high potential rewards – no previous experience necessary.

The initial interview was with a nasty little sales manager who, had I not been so naïve, should have put me off straight away. He engaged me on the spot with glowing promises of substantial commission and rapid promotion which could be all mine after two weeks with one of their best representatives. That worthy turned out to be a stocky little Irishman with a command of English that was not overly impressive. I was bidden to follow him on his rounds and study his doorstep technique for a few days before having a go myself.

There were problems with education in working class districts of London at this time; most schools had large classes and a shortage of teachers. But imagine my surprise when my mentor opened his pitch to our first flat-dwelling potential customer by saying that we were calling about the over-crowding in schools. He then went into an extraordinary routine in which he pointed to an editor's name in his folder, saying rather grandly, 'This is the individual.' Then there was a pregnant pause during which he made no attempt to explain who or what that individual was. 'He has put it into four,' he then added. I could never understand why no one ever asked, 'Four what?', but they didn't. When I queried this later I was told that, should it happen, I must never mention the dread word 'Books' at that stage or the sale would be dead.

We usually managed to get into the house fairly quickly, where the hard sell began, and then came the part where the well-intentioned parent would be required to sign an agreement to pay a very substantial sum of money over a very long period.

By this stage I had firmly formed the opinion that what we were doing might not be illegal but was undoubtedly highly immoral. Unfortunately it was all too easy, as I found when the time came for me to go solo. After a few days I had already achieved several sales, though with increasing misgivings about the whole thing. I began to feel physically ill and became increasingly reluctant to try any further. Pamela was inclined quite justifiably to put this down to incipient laziness until she came out with me one evening and saw for herself the poverty of the people in the target area and the ease with which they could be gulled into parting with far more than they could afford, in the pathetic belief that the presence in their homes of a few books would somehow guarantee their offspring an escape to better things.

Eventually I went back to see the obnoxious sales manager and told him that I despised what was going on and no longer wished to be a part of it. At first he attempted to cajole me into continuing by telling me how well I was doing and how impressive my figures were. Then he grew a little nastier, suggesting that my 'training' had cost the company a lot of money and I was therefore under some obligation to repay them. Finally the message got through that I meant what I said and he abruptly paid me off and tersely dismissed me.

Miraculously, I immediately felt better.

Once again unemployed, I suddenly remembered that two or three years previously I had been given the name and address of the head of the foreign section of Dutch overseas radio in Hilversum. Why this information had remained in my wallet I shall never know, but there it was and this seemed a good time to make use of it. I wrote at once to Frits Thors in Hilversum and shortly received an invitation to submit an audition. In those days they had an agreement with HMV in Oxford Street where applicants for

[85]

jobs could go and record direct on to an acetate disc a reading from a newspaper and an example of introducing a music programme.

My performance must have met the required standard and I was rapidly offered a two year contract with Radio Nederland Wereldomroep English Department. We were told that we would be accommodated in a hotel near the radio station until such time as we could find an apartment of our own. We accepted at once and in November set off to start our new life.

Hilversum today has developed into a vast urban sprawl that virtually joins up with Amsterdam on one side and Utrecht on the other, but in the early fifties it had the atmosphere of a small country town surrounded by farmland, woods and lakes. It was nevertheless the broadcasting centre of Holland, where radio had started in the early twenties with a short-wave station that had the call sign PCJ and a regular programme, introduced by Eddie Startz, with the rather quaint title of 'The Happy Station'. Eddie is no longer with us, but astonishingly the programme survives.

The thirties saw the development and expansion of domestic medium-wave broadcasting based in buildings of the most avant garde architecture for their time. These were owned by companies financed by monthly subscription from listeners through the purchase of stamps at the post office. When I lived in Holland there were four of these, controlled by the Labour and Liberal parties, by the Nonconformist and the Roman Catholic church; they were known respectively as AVRO, VARA, NCRV and KRO. PCJ had developed into a fully fledged overseas short-wave service, financed by the government; it broadcast in Dutch, English, Spanish, French, Indonesian and Arabic. It was based in three separate, formerly private, large houses; one was the headquarters and offices, one was the news department, and the other contained studios. Equipment for all five organisations was provided by a shared facility called Netherlands Radio Union.

The head of the English section was a friendly chap called Emil van Dulken who had learned his English mainly from American

[86]

movies, with the result that he had a marked American accent and a predilection for being addressed as 'Van'. With my arrival he had a team of five broadcasters: Mike and Ron who were both Canadians, Walt from the States and Robin, an Englishman who had been an organist at York Minster. There was also a secretary whose real Dutch name had long since been forgotten because Robin had christened her 'Flossie', with which sobriquet she seemed content.

Between us we compiled daily a forty minute programme which always comprised a news bulletin, an outside broadcast report from somewhere in Holland and a short musical item. This was then transmitted three times in every twenty-four hours, beamed to different parts of the world. As I soon developed a liking for and hopefully some degree of skill in interviews and commentaries I tended to spend much of my time on the road travelling the length and breadth of the country, though I still had to cover the occasional middle of the night transmission and take my turn at compiling a weekly magazine called 'Window on Holland' which was a compendium of extracts from the week's reports.

The first surprise came when I discovered that all recordings made through the outside broadcast van were cut straight to disc and those discs were used for transmissions. We did occasionally and reluctantly have recourse to a tape recorder the like of which I have thankfully never encountered elsewhere. It was called a Maihak and had a clockwork motor which had to be wound up before recording. Unfortunately it was prone to run down without any warning, turning one's voice to a drawl which you only discovered when transferring the recording to disc for broadcast purposes. Later on, of course, tapes became more commonplace for all aspects of the work, which gave us much more flexibility and ease of editing. Though, strangely enough, some four years later when I joined the BBC, acetate discs were still used to insert reports into the programme 'Radio Newsreel'. We would mark the portions for broadcast with a yellow chinagraph pencil; the studio managers had to acquire great dexterity in making what were known as jump cuts, live on air, from sentence to sentence.

In the reporting wagon, where there would usually be representatives from all of the sections, the common language was almost invariably Dutch. It therefore became necessary to learn that tongue as quickly as possible. In my case this was not too difficult since there are many similarities, in both vocabulary and grammar, with German which I had spent eight years learning at school. The odd thing was that after a while, when I attempted to speak Dutch in Holland people thought I was German, and when attempting German on a visit over the border I was taken for Dutch!

On arrival in Hilversum Pamela and I had been taken to a pleasant little hotel in a quiet tree-lined street called Melkpad where for the first time we came across the Dutch breakfast of cold meat, cheese, rusks and jam so unfamiliar to English taste. In these days of package holidays this continental meal has become much more familiar of course, but in the fifties it came as quite a surprise.

In retrospect I realise what a hard time this must have been for Pamela. I had the interest of the work to occupy me and through it met many people every day. She was quite alone; she knew no one to start with, and was not able to pick up the language anything like so quickly. Other members of the staff were extremely friendly and there was soon a good deal of entertaining going on which eased the problem, but the first weeks were very difficult for her.

We soon found a good-sized room with a conservatory in a house owned by a large rosy-cheeked friendly lady whose name was Mrs Vos. She spoke little or no English, but entertained us regularly to tea in her own cosy room; bit by bit we came to understand and to be very fond of each other. In her quarters we first encountered the Dutch tea cosy, which opened at the top with a snap fastener, like a purse. It was effective, but it also led to a strong, stewed brew which neither of us has ever liked. The furniture was all very heavy and dark and we noticed that it was the custom to cover tables with material more like a carpet than a cloth.

The only trouble with our new home was that it was also occupied by mice. This particularly affected me as I inherited a sort of mouse phobia from my mother which I have never been able to conquer. After I had returned from one of the late transmissions one night Pamela woke up and was amazed to find me sitting in bed pitching shoes and slippers into the middle of the room where I had seen one of the little perishers sitting up washing his whiskers.

Soon after our arrival we encountered one of the pleasanter Dutch customs. The celebration of Sinta Klaas was new to us. It is similar to the English Christmas but is held on the fifth of December; it is the children's festival and the time for parties and presents, while Christmas itself is reserved for the Christian festival.

Sinta Klaas is the familiar name for St Nicholas, who annually arrives in the heart of Amsterdam by boat, accompanied by his little black servant, Zwaarte Piet. They then visit children, like Father Christmas, by descending chimneys to leave sweets in the clogs left in the hearth.

Our first Sinta Klaas was a real designer job, with seasonal snow, pretty street decorations and lights, and the inevitable street organs, 'draaiorgels', playing folksongs and carols. There were, too, the foodstuffs traditionally eaten at this time – gingerbread men and the wonderful 'oliebollen', a sort of doughnut served hot.

No doubt much of this has changed and gone, though on a visit to friends just a couple of years ago in late November I was delighted to be taken to a huge marquee on a village green, and there we enjoyed pancakes and syrup waffles to the music of a mechanical organ. The magic still worked and joy was unconfined.

Not long after that Christmas of 1952, while I was still very much a rooky reporter, there occurred a national disaster of great magnitude. In the southern part of the country the unthinkable happened and the retaining dykes were breached by storm, flooding vast areas and costing many lives. A huge rescue and restoration programme was launched and teams of American and British servicemen came in from Germany to help.

As the waters were gradually pushed back again I was able to get through with a reporting car to broadcast commentaries on the scenes in Schouwen Duiveland. Houses were ruined and bare trees had branches draped with weed and flotsam. A strange sight and a feeling, which I remember describing, as though we were still under water although the sea had gone.

Eventually nearly all of the flooded land had been reclaimed once again and there remained just one gap in a dyke before the final pumping out could begin. The technique was to float huge concrete caissons into the gaps, to open sea cocks and sink them in place and then to fill them with sandbags, thus making a new section of wall. The final closure, attended by Queen Juliana, was to take place in the middle of the night, as dictated by the tides. The time coincided exactly with our English transmission, and it fell to my lot to provide the commentary. Thank goodness I had swatted up every available document about the resources and methods to be employed because, despite the most meticulous attention to detail, things didn't quite go according to plan.

I travelled by car as near as possible to the centre of operations, then had to proceed by small boat to the point where the crucial caisson was to be sunk. Thereafter, I climbed by ladder from the boat on to the lip of a caisson that was already in place and that was to be my commentary position. Unfortunately I slipped when transferring from the top of the ladder and although I just managed to grab the top of the structure I was climbing I nevertheless dislocated my thumb in the process. A technician caught me under the arms and hauled me to comparative safety.

My damaged hand was hastily strapped up in a make-shift sling, and a microphone thrust into the other one. The time for my transmission arrived and I went on air expecting to provide a commentary for ten to fifteen minutes. At the end of the first quarter of an hour there was no sign that the historic moment was upon us, and I received a scrawled note, 'Carry on'. This was repeated several times; in the end I remained on air for an hour and twenty minutes before the exercise was completed and the night was filled with celebratory hooters and klaxons.

It was of course a privilege to have been the broadcaster chosen to cover this momentous event, and as far as I am aware the recording of that commentary lies to this day in the Wereldomroep archives. But there is a funny little coda to the story. I had been walking on air for days after the event, congratulated by my colleagues and fully persuaded that I had done a good job. Then came the one and only listener reaction. A postcard from someone in India saying, 'I hear transmission on this day and hear man talking about water, water, water.'

[12]

The Dutch gulden is today one of the strongest currencies in Europe, but in the early fifties the exchange rate was ten to the pound so that we were quite comfortably off on what was a fairly modest salary in English terms. In addition there were numerous extras available which really put the icing on the cake. For the most part these were voice overs for commercials or commentaries for documentary films; I also got to act in a couple of episodes of a spy serial which was being made for American television.

A producer from the States had brought the actor Robert Alda over to an Amsterdam studio to star in this series, which otherwise used Dutch actors to play all the Europeans in the stories. The producer couldn't believe his luck when he discovered at a radio station an Englishman who had been an actor and had actually appeared at the Old Vic!

On our first encounter he was quite overcome by the fact that I was able to understand him so readily and could play to camera or not as he required. 'Gee, you're a great actor,' he told me at every take, and promptly booked me to appear in the next episode.

Unfortunately, this part demanded that I should not only drive a car, which at that stage I couldn't, but even worse that I should drive it full tilt at someone else, leaving it to his dexterity to get out of the way. After several ineffective takes during which I either stalled the car, or couldn't bring myself to drive anything like fast enough, the words of praise had changed to, 'Jesus! You mighta bin a great actor at the Old Vic, but yer a goddam lousy driver.'

He solved the problem by pulling a cap down over his eyes and driving the car himself, then having me taken out on location where I had my first experience of cutaway shots: close-ups of me at the wheel, driving sedately down an empty road, to be edited into the action shots later.

There was no such easy solution to another scene in which a Canadian colleague from Wereldomroep played a corpse being conveyed in a wooden crate on a horse-drawn wagon. The wagon was halted by German soldiers and the crate thrown from the cart so that the lid fell off. Close-up of Ken, deceased, in the box. Unfortunately at the very moment the director called for the camera to roll, the horse felt the need to relieve itself in most spectacular fashion and there lay Ken, with eyes closed, while an amber torrent cascaded all around him.

On a rather more cerebral plane I was engaged to record commentaries for a medical unit at Utrecht University which made instructional films for world-wide distribution. The director of these asked me whether I was squeamish about the sight of blood, as he had previously had the experience of commentators either fainting or being sick in the recording booth. I assured him that I would be all right, but it was a salutary warning on his part as there were several instances when I felt, to say the least, queasy.

The first film to upset me recorded a cancer patient; an operation had removed much of one side of his face, including one eye and cheek. This meant that it was possible to film and record the movements of his uvula as he spoke. The director then wanted me to synchronise speech to these movements. It is of course common practice to add 'lip-synch' recordings in one language to screen performances in another, but I very much doubt whether anyone had ever been asked to do 'uvula-synch' before. When we had completed the film, I asked what had become of the patient. 'Oh, he died,' was the callously casual response.

The other documentary which made me take a tight hold on myself was a film shot in colour of an operation to separate Siamese twins, joined at the hip; they shared a common liver. Happily in this instance everything was concluded successfully and the film was a

[93]

great success in medical schools, I understand; I was rather proud of being associated with this unusual exercise.

Another opportunity which afforded a great deal of extra work for both Pamela and myself has had the bonus of forging lifelong links with a family as close to us now as any of our own kin.

One of the translators in the newsroom at the radio station was an Irishman, John Warren, who had been a regular army officer promoted to very high rank at an early age while serving in India. He was as brilliant a linguist as I have ever encountered, remarkably fluent in many tongues. Because of his knowledge of several Indian dialects he was posted to Berlin at the end of the war to seek out and interrogate Asian deserters of which, it seems, there were a great many.

Not long after this, John met and married a Dutch girl named Helene, and in due course they had three children. He left the army and joined the radio as a news translator; he also ran a private translation business from home which eventually became his full-time occupation. It was a great asset to him to have Pamela's services as a typist for the enormous amount of work that flooded in, and I was also able to help, correcting the English in some of the initial drafts.

Sadly, John was also an epileptic and this led to his death at an early age, leaving Helene with the three young children, Ric, short for Patrick, Mieke, a Dutch short form for Mary Ann, and Suellen. They are now, of course, grown, with children of their own and have all visited us in our home in Kent. Mieke, especially, came to us for the summer every year from the age of twelve until she married for the first time. That union resulted in the birth of two lovely boys, and a girl was adopted before the marriage came to an end. Now she has a marvellous husband and another baby girl whom she kindly allows us to regard as a grandchild. Both of the boys and the elder girl have followed in their mother's footsteps and spent holidays with us, I hope to the benefit of their English, though that was already quite remarkable.

I was also honoured to be asked to stand *in loco parentis* at the

[94]

second wedding and to give my adored Mieke away. It seems to have amused most of the wedding guests that I was at least able to begin my speech at the reception in Dutch.

As a result of the reasonable affluence we enjoyed from broadcasting, translating, filming and all, we were soon able to buy our first ever car. It was a remarkable vehicle: a DKW two-stroke, made in Germany before the war as a cheap, people's car and so a forerunner of the Volkswagen Beetle. It had quite a stylish line and was exceedingly simple mechanically, with three forward gears and reverse operated by an angled handle on the dashboard.

I soon became adept at changing wheels, since punctures were fairly commonplace, and I also learned to clean the carburettor, but that was the full extent of my know-how. Still, breakdowns aside, the great advantage of this car was the way it extended our mobility, which had hitherto been restricted to the range of the inevitable Dutch bicycle. It also had another use with the arrival of our son. There were many times when he showed no inclination to sleep at all, but with his carry cot placed on the back seat it only needed a couple of laps around the block and he was away.

We were able to have both sets of grandparents over to visit us, and our farming friends Joan and George. Everyone was taken to the famous tourist places, Volendam and the island of Maarken, last bastions of the traditional costumes, and was dutifully photographed there in same, looking idiotically phoney. Goodness knows how many miles that little car travelled, but it eventually blew up beyond repair and had to be sold off for scrap.

Our son Christopher was quite decidedly planned and was born on January 27, 1954 in the Roman Catholic Hospital in Hilversum. We were not of that faith, but our friend Helene was, and rather tended to get us organised. Pamela says that in the extremes of labour she frequently had recourse to bellowing 'Oh God!' with feeling, and was aware that the nursing sisters, who were all nuns, were clacking away with their beads in defence of her mortal soul. Or perhaps of their own.

Our physician, Dr de Groot, had recommended that I take

advantage of the opportunity, not then in vogue in England, of being present at the birth. I was glad that I took his advice, but Pamela thought it was a bit strong when, after a successful delivery, he congratulated me on being particularly courageous. 'Blooming cheek,' she said. 'What about me? I had the child.'

So now we were three, and before the arrival of the DKW car, regularly followed a common Dutch method of transport about the streets of Hilversum. I rode a bicycle, while Pamela sat on a rack over the rear wheel and towed the pram containing Christopher behind her. It sounds horrific today, I know, but I promise you it was not an unusual sight at that time. The car had entered our lives not a moment too soon.

TV's 'Thank Your Lucky Stars' (early '60s). Clockwise from left:
Ray Ellington, self, Pete Murray, Philip Jones (director), Bernard Cribbins, Danny Williams,
Susan Maughan, Joyce Blair, Adam Faith

'Lucky Stars' again. 'Hi there, guys and gals'. Jimmy Savile kindly lent me the jacket but I had to provide the cigar

In the ring with singing American wrestler Frankie Townsend

On honeymoon with Pamela in Oxfordshire, 1951

With my parents in Volendam, Holland 1953 . . .

. . . the year before this young man appeared:
Christopher, aged about two weeks

Hitherto unpublished Beatles pictures. I took them myself in Chicago, 1963

With Dame Vera Lynn, John
Dankworth and Frankie
Vaughan at a RFH charity
concert

As the anguished Percy
Winthrop in *Rattle of a Simple
Man* at Bromley, with Pamela as
Cyrenne

With Pepe, the kitten given me by a 'Lucky Stars' fan

A rare moment of quiet before the pandemonium of 'Lucky Stars'

Presenting Kenny Ball with a gold disc for 'Midnight in Moscow' at the
Playhouse Theatre

With Bobby Vee (right) and his group, The V Men

A real band of DJs.
From left: Steve Race, congas; Alan Dell, bass; Ken Sykora, guitar; Jack Jackson, trumpet;
David Gell, drums; Jimmy Young, piano; Don Moss, tambourine; self, valve trombone;
and Sam Costa, piano

[13]

The end of two years in Holland came all too quickly for me and I think that, for my own part, by the end of 1954 I might have settled down there permanently, but what a lot I should have missed if Pamela hadn't decided that she wanted Christopher to be brought up in England.

It did mean, of course, that we were once again out of work and by this time had no very clear idea of what we wanted to do, beyond deciding that we were no longer in a position to gamble on trying to get back into the theatre. The obvious thing seemed to be to attempt to get into the BBC as an announcer, so an application for an audition was submitted. Meanwhile, through contacts in Holland I was introduced to the Dutch Embassy in London who employed me to translate a technical book of the kind my friend John Warren had churned out day after day. With my far less fluent command of the language it was a very hard chore, but I struggled through to the end. I don't think the result was very good and I was certainly never asked to do another one.

We then moved up to stay with my parents in Coventry and I began to investigate all manner of possibilities. One interview was with the rubber manufacturing company, Dunlop, who were looking for someone to edit their house magazine. I'd never done anything of that sort, but they seemed reasonably impressed with my journalistic experience in radio and said they would bear me in mind.

I then had the thought of applying to Jaguar for a job as a salesman, thinking that a reasonable knowledge of French, German and Dutch might be an asset. There couldn't have been all that many people walking into the employment office of the factory in Brown's Lane, Coventry, with those credentials and ambitions, so a rather puzzled receptionist asked me to wait. For quite a long time. And then I was told apologetically that the sales force was recruited from younger men (good heavens, I was twenty-six!) who had first to gain experience on the shop floor.

Leaving the works gates a touch dejected, I saw immediately opposite a small dairy displaying a notice announcing vacancies for a pasteuriser and for deliverymen. Further investigation proved that they were far less demanding on this side of the road and in no time flat I was taken on. For the next six months I was a milkman.

My first job was to drive a lorry with bulk deliveries to cafés and workshops in the city, then to run out to a few outlying farms to pick up churns of fresh milk and finally to work in the dairy alongside the chief pasteuriser in an attempt to learn the finer points of his craft. He first removed the churn lid and then, after a thoughtful sniff or two, would tell me what those particular cows had been eating. All I can remember is that if it had been kale, then the milk smelled rather nasty before treatment.

It was just my luck that this part of my life should coincide with another pretty severe winter, so that cycling to work at five thirty each morning was not pleasant and driving a truck on icy roads was even less so.

I also discovered at the cost of a strained muscle or two that a ten gallon churn, full, is rather heavy and lifting it on to a lorry at about waist height a fairly exhausting process.

Similarly, in the dairy, each day's work ended with stacking crates of bottles for the next day's delivery into a cold storage room. Each crate contained thirty bottles and they were stacked ten crates high. Two hefty young colleagues threw them around two at a time which initially I found impossible, until they kindly showed me the knack of carrying them with arms stretched straight down then, at the last moment, snatching them up to chest level and sliding them on to the stack. Not an exercise I relished or recommend but I suppose it was as beneficial as weight-lifting. I was certainly very fit at this time.

I lived in the hope of hearing of other jobs and in the meantime applied direct to BBC producer Jack Dabbs who for many years was responsible for jazz gramophone record programmes, including a series called 'World of Jazz'. To my surprised delight he accepted my suggestion of a programme on Dutch jazz and I travelled to London to make the recording. The following week, after the broadcast, a delivery girl in the dairy regarded me with a newfound respect and said, 'Cor, we've got a bloody star workin' with us!'

Someone as inexperienced and undedicated as I was had to cause a minor disaster and it came when I was ordered to take out a small van and collect three extra churns from a farm as quickly as possible. Picking them up was no problem and getting them on to a much lower tailboard was easy, too. The hitch occurred when I roared back to base, swung into the drive at a colossal rate and tipped over all three churns, spilling the whole thirty gallons.

I approached the boss cap in hand, with desperate apologies, and asked if he would consider stopping an amount from my wages weekly until I had paid for the loss. This truly Christian man kept very calm and said that as I had been honest with him and offered to make restitution he would put it down to experience and not require me to pay for it.

Even such treatment, I'm afraid, didn't make the work any more congenial in my eyes and as I didn't seem to be getting anywhere with other job applications I wrote to Holland once more and asked if they would be prepared to take me back at the radio station.

At the dairy, after a few months, another man was taken on to cover the work I had been doing and I was transferred to a daily delivery round. This was physically less strenuous but the working day seemed to go on a lot longer. There was also an aspect that I would never have thought about; several elderly customers, living alone, were obviously so desperately lonely that they looked to the milkman's call as a highlight of their day, asking him in for a cup of tea and trying to detain him as long as possible with conversation, oblivious to the fact that he probably had umpteen other calls to make.

And, yes, indeed, the music hall joke of the bored housewife hoping to find moments of comfort with the milkman is, sadly, based on fact. I experienced the rather forlorn invitations but am pleased to be able to add that compassion did not lead to temptation.

Then, eventually, I came not so much to another of life's crossroads as a roundabout with exits in all directions. The jobs I had been seeking for months all came up within a two week period.

First to arrive was an offer from Holland to return to Wereldomroep with the elevated status of assistant head of the English section. As a further inducement they offered us a flat in one of the blocks built exclusively for Dutch national radio employees. My immediate reaction was to accept this generous gesture and a date was fixed for our return.

Then Dunlop came through out of the blue and said they had decided I was just the person to edit their magazine. When would I like to start?

And then, of course, the BBC also decided that my audition with them had been satisfactory and they offered me a post as trainee announcer.

In view of Pamela's preferences it was no contest. I withdrew from the agreement to return to Holland, told Dunlop that another post had come up in the interim, and said farewell to the dairy.

Although television was under way in 1955, relatively few people had receivers and working for the BBC meant very much working for sound radio. Suddenly I was meeting and talking to Olympian beings whose names had been familiar to me since my childhood: Stuart Hibbard, John Snagge, Frank Phillips and Alvar Liddell, to name but a few. No longer wearing dinner jackets to read the news on the wireless, it's true, but still steeped in Reithian formalities to a degree. Huge changes were imminent and I was to play a part in them, but not for a year or two.

Daily broadcasting then was through the Home Service, the Light Programme and the Third Programme and it was more than likely that one would be required to spend some time at Oxford Street, home of the General Overseas Service, and at Bush House where foreign language broadcasts and an English European Service were transmitted. Each service had its own team of announcers and in the mid fifties very few people managed to cross over from one service to another.

I was told when I joined that, despite my experience in Forces Radio and in Holland, it was considered that I would benefit from a month's course at the staff training department in the Marylebone Road; it was designed to prepare studio managers. It seemed to me at first that this was an irritating delay with little or no purpose to it, but I was wrong about that and I have never ceased to be thankful for the experience.

The first few days were devoted to lectures on the basics of studio layout, with schematic drawings showing how to set up for a transmission, linking microphones via a jack field to a control desk which might also be coupled to gramophones and tape machines. We were inaugurated into the mysteries of the various types of mikes available at that period and learned their suitability for different aspects of broadcasting.

Then we moved on to practical work, with much concentration on the finer points of playing records. These were almost exclusively of the 78 r.p.m. variety and, as I have mentioned previously, were still widely used to carry reports in news programmes. One listened on headphones to find the first words to be broadcast then stopped the turntable. On a cue from the narrator or news reader one then had to 'spin in' the turntable and with the other hand open a fader on the front of the gram deck, play the required passage and on the out cue fade out again quickly. The exercise fiendishly devised to encourage dexterity in this technique consisted of a conversation with alternate lines recorded on separate discs, so that while one was playing the other could be set up. To make it harder, the lines became progressively shorter, reducing to no more than two words – you were then in the realms of luck and guesswork.

No real-life situation was ever quite as demanding as that, but I had already met several tricky situations along these lines in Germany. For example, we sometimes put out half hour plays recorded on several sides of ten inch 78s, and the last words of each side were duplicated at the beginning of the next. You had about twenty seconds to get them running in synchronisation and then with a flick of two faders to change over from one side to the next. That was called the overlap changeover. Then there was the butt change, in which one followed a script and on reaching the final word at the end of a side spun in the next side. How on earth it ever came about I can't imagine, but a poor duty announcer once came across a butt change on which the changeover word had been split between two sides, something like, 'Well, all right if you say so, but neverthe . . .' (end of side one) '. . . less,' (start of side two). The poor man turned white. He knew only one announcer in Hamburg who could almost be guaranteed to get it right and that was

Sergeant Jimmy Kingsbury, later to do much accomplished work at the BBC, especially becloaked and bemonocled on 'Friday Night is Music Night'. Fortunately Jimmy was available on this occasion and sure enough, performed the changeover flawlessly.

At the end of the Marylebone course the other five or six trainees all went off to spend three months in domestic broadcasting and three in the overseas service. Someone thought I should follow suit, albeit as an announcer.

All posts at the BBC were and I believe still are advertised internally and from the applicants some are then chosen to confront a board and they choose, as it were, a winner. As a trainee announcer, one was expected to apply for the first announcing post to come up, regardless of which service it might be with. I had set my sights on the Light Programme, since that was the home of most of the 'entertainment' shows with which I wanted to become involved.

I was sent first of all, however, to the General Overseas Service based, as I have mentioned, in Oxford Street in the basement of a large store. There I was told that I should be sent to shadow someone in a continuity suite for a few days before being required to fly solo. It was a surprise to find in the studio none other than Robin Simpson, the former York Minster organist whom I had known for a while in Hilversum. He had left Holland under a bit of a cloud; he had shown himself once too often prone to the familiar broadcaster's dilemma of a fondness for raising the elbow. The problem appeared not to have diminished to any noticeable extent and he soon departed from the BBC as well. I certainly never met him again after that brief acquaintance. A great shame, for he had a fine voice and when in full possession of his wits and faculties was an excellent broadcaster.

After a few weeks with the General Overseas Service I was sent to Bush House to work with the European Service and although I have often met many colleagues who profess to love working in that area of broadcasting I must say that for me it represented the epitome of boredom and I couldn't wait to get out. Fortunately, after only about a couple of weeks I was sent to Broadcasting House to work in domestic broadcasting.

My first attachment was to the Home Service where I was assigned to a team that was headed by Frank Phillips and another senior announcer, Robin Holmes, who was a delightful man. At the end of the day, Frank would go off to Alexandra Palace to read the closedown news bulletin for television, Robin read the news for Home Service, and I closed down the Light Programme continuity. Then, on Frank's return to Broadcasting House, we assembled in his office for gossip and a bottle of whisky, retiring at an ungodly hour to be woken not long after, me to read the Fat Stock prices and Robin the news.

It was not long before I was considered suitable myself to become a Home Service news reader. It was an honour to be among such distinguished company, but it was also a nerve-racking job. After reporting to the newsroom in Egton House, next door to Broadcasting House, I would collect the first page or so of a bulletin from a duty sub editor and then go into a huddle with a member of the pronunciation unit to be briefed on the correct way to utter especially difficult, usually foreign, words and names. After that, it was off to the news studio, designated 3G at that time, there to start reading the pages. I would be joined later by the sub with the remainder of the bulletin, and pray that it would not contain too many hurdles insurmountable without aid from the afore-mentioned pronunciation unit.

The head of presentation in my day was Andrew Timothy, father of actor Christopher now famous for his portrayal of the vet James Herriot. Andrew had himself been a distinguished announcer; he was also famous for having appeared on the Goon Show. He always monitored news bulletins, and woe betide anyone guilty of sottish solecisms. I still remember being summoned to his office one morning after reading the previous night's nine o'clock news.

'How do you pronounce this?' he asked, pushing across a piece of paper bearing the word 'revolver'. I got it right.

'Then why', barked Andrew, 'did you say "revohlver" last

night? Don't be a clot and think what you're doing next time.'

As a coda to that story I must emphasise that Andrew was a warm and friendly man, a real professional, who quite rightly demanded from staff his own high standards. In recent years, whenever I have interviewed actor son Christopher he has always conveyed greetings from 'the old man'.

I was also lucky enough in my period as an announcer to have the benefit of working with a speech specialist widely known as 'Fanny' McCloud. Even when no longer a trainee one was sent to Miss McCloud for occasional sessions to keep one up to scratch with enunciation as well as pronunciation. Severe she certainly was at times, but always immensely helpful. There would appear to be no one working in her capacity at the BBC today – more's the pity in my view.

I never worked with any regularity on the Third Programme, but did do occasional continuity shifts and announced a few recitals from studios in Maida Vale. On one occasion, when reading an announcement written by someone else I must have made a pig's ear of pronouncing 'exegesis'. Whatever I said, there followed a little later a vitriolic letter from an Oxford don abusing me and berating the Corporation for employing me. And damn me, I still don't know how to say the wretched word!

One memory of the Third Programme I shall always treasure. I was announcing a very strange concert of contemporary German music from one of the studios in Maida Vale. The composer himself conducted a small group of musicians and some eight or nine singers; the broadcast was live. I rang Pamela after a rehearsal and told her that the 'music' consisted of the weirdest collection of grunts, groans and bongs imaginable; when I got home she told me she had listened, assuming that I had been exaggerating grossly, only to discover that my description had been extremely accurate.

The great joy from my point of view, however, and one that I couldn't possibly share with listeners, was that as the work jerked along so the composer/conductor's trousers began to fall down. As the programme was live on air he couldn't possibly stop and had to add to his repertoire of already bizarre gestures a series of frantic grabs at his waistline to hoist back the wayward garment.

On a happier occasion I had to announce a concert with the BBC Symphony Orchestra conducted by Sir Malcolm Sargent before a small invited audience in the largest of the Maida Vale studios, the Number One. Sir Malcolm emerged from the conductor's room, immaculate as ever, and walked straight over to my desk. He smiled, introduced himself to this very timid and nervous announcer and asked if there was any way in which he could help me before the broadcast began.

I have in more recent years heard many people, usually musicians, say harsh things about Sir Malcolm but for that one kind gesture to me I have always defended him to the hilt.

Although the majority of those who have earned a living by introducing important events publicly on the radio sound relaxed and at ease I think most of us are often screwed up inside with anxiety over the possibility of getting things wrong. The very process of trying to hide this tension can have far-reaching effects. This story, about the late Alvar Liddell, illustrates the point.

Before I joined the BBC the news-reading set up was apparently a little different from the one that I was to know. Two duplicate booths, with microphones, were situated on either side of another compartment; communication to both of them was possible through hatches. The announcer would go into whichever booth he was directed to while the sub editor fed him sheets of news through the appropriate hatch.

On the occasion of this story, Alvar had completed his shift for the day and repaired to the announcers' common room where, because he was Swedish and because it was full moon, or for whatever reason, he was making frequent use of a bottle of schnapps. As time went by he grew more and more pale and tight-lipped and glanced with greater regularity at the clock on the wall. After a while his behaviour began to cause some concern among those of his colleagues also in the room.

Then as the clock neared the time for the next news bulletin to be read, Alvar stood up and marched solemnly to the suite of booths. Entering one of them, he sat staring woodenly at the clock until its hands were in the appointed place and then said, 'Fuck, fuck, fuck, fuck. And I don't care if I do get the fucking sack.' He was not, happily, in the 'on air' booth and so escaped any penalty, continuing to give delight with his wonderful presentation for many years to come.

When the time eventually came for me to leave announcing and transfer for a while to production John Snagge told me that I was making a wise move. 'The vocational announcer', John remarked, 'is a rare bird. Only Stuart Hibberd, Frank Phillips and Alvar Liddell deserve the description in my view.' I think he was probably right.

I mentioned the possibility of penalties for misdemeanours in announcing and although such punishment occurred infrequently the form it took could be rather odd. A classic example of this came about when the highly popular Jack de Manio was reading a bulletin and, I have no doubt inadvertently, pronounced the name of the river Niger as 'Nigger', thereby upsetting sensibilities in certain quarters. For this he was suspended, on full pay, for three months. A whole quarter's holiday with pay always seemed to me to offer more in the way of temptation than warning.

Not that the aforementioned 'pay' amounted to very much in the mid fifties. It's astonishing to reflect now that during this probationary period I was paid fourteen pounds a week, with no opportunity of earning any extra as had been the case in Holland. Furthermore, one had to sign an agreement with the Corporation that one would live within reasonable travelling distance of one's place of employment to ensure one's presence as required at all times. To be honest I think it had already become necessary to turn a blind eye to that particular clause in the contract since most accommodation within reasonable distance of Broadcasting House was already in high rental areas.

We had had the good fortune to find ourselves a large and roomy flat in Willesden, with several rooms on a ground floor and semi-basement. There was even a garden accessible by climbing through one of the basement windows. This highly desirable residence, once decorated and albeit sparsely furnished with whatever we could beg or borrow, cost us five pounds a week and therefore left very little for food, clothes and other household expenses. Fortunately I could get to all of the studio premises then in use either by bus or tube and indeed Maida Vale was within energetic walking distance.

I was in those days a smoker but by resorting to 'roll your own' tobacco that outlay was kept down; as another economy I would often take sandwiches to work. There is a decided piquancy now in remembering that young man with the posh voice saying 'This is the BBC Home Service', and then digging into the cheese and pickle followed by canteen coffee and a roll-up.

Christopher had by this time grown out of babyhood and become a lovely golden-haired little boy who was extremely mobile. Indeed he was always a fast developer physically, pulling himself to his feet at seven months of age and walking very early. He had now taken with relish to a three-wheeler bicycle on which he led us on our shopping expeditions. He also enjoyed the garden in which he spent many happy hours with spade, bucket and water. This water was in an old zinc bath and one day Chris called up to his mother at the kitchen window, 'Mummy, there's a 'pider in the bath.' This bloated creature turned out on inspection to be a drowned mouse. Pamela, quite rightly, saw this as a health hazard and ordered me on my return to remove the offending corpse. It will have become apparent by now that this was hardly going to rate very highly on my list of favourite occupations, but even so Pamela wasn't ready for the lengths to which I would go to avoid personal contact even with a dead rodent. She had suggested that the very best way of removing the body was to bury it, but after a protracted absence on my part, she looked out to find that I had dug a deep pit in the garden and was about to bury not only the mouse but also the bath in which it floated. I suppose it was a bit much, really.

We were not destined to stay in this Willesden flat for very long but long enough, nevertheless, to provide us with one inexplicable experience which has exercised our imaginations – and those of others – ever since.

The main entrance to the house and to our own flat front door was up a flight of steps from the front garden. In front of our basement window there was also a path going round to a side door to which a few steps led down. One winter's morning, after a night of quite heavy snowfall, we awoke to find footprints in one direction only leading from the front steps round to our side entrance, which was never used and where the door was kept permanently locked. I'll bet that would have got old Poirot going a bit, not to mention Sherlock Holmes.

After just over two frugal but mainly happy years we went to visit friends in Orpington who had told us of some new houses that had been built in the nearby village of Chelsfield. We saw the show house and decided immediately that it was just what we wanted. Although we have had one other change of home we have stayed in this part of Kent for the past thirty-three years.

Needless to say there had been an increase of salary before we decided to become mortgage payers; this stemmed mainly from my progress from trainee to full time staff member. To my temporary horror a vacancy had cropped up in the World Service which I very definitely did not want, so I ignored the rules and refused to apply for it. Fortunately there was very shortly afterwards another opening in the Light Programme which I certainly did want and happily got.

[15]

At last I found myself in the midst of the kind of entertainment which at that stage of my life I most enjoyed. The Light Programme was the main home for dance and jazz bands, for brass and military bands and for some of the finest comedy shows that British radio has ever produced.

In a very short space of time I made the acquaintance of a man my father had known well during his own days as a brass bandsman, Harry Mortimer. He was still a very active conductor at the peak of his profession, although he had by this time given up playing cornet and trumpet and was the Head of the BBC Brass and Military Band department. Our first encounter was an odd one, for I introduced myself and explained the connection, but Harry unaccountably denied any knowledge of my father. This despite the fact that Joe had been an adjudicator at a Crystal Palace contest when Harry first conducted there and the young Mortimer had actually asked my father for advice before this event.

In later years, when I taxed Harry with this lapse of memory he refused to believe it had ever happened. He certainly made amends by getting Joe a ticket for the Royal Albert Hall at a national contest final when they had long been sold out.

The relationship was eventually fulfilled for me when Harry reached his seventy-fifth birthday and I was asked to write the script for the celebratory concert broadcast in his honour; he was presented with a bound copy. He continued to visit the studios into his eighties and I had the pleasure of interviewing him on numerous occasions. He had a marvellous sense of humour that was enhanced by his dry Yorkshire wit and of course he had a fund of anecdotes about his years with the bands.

My chief delight, however, was in working with the famous dance bands and orchestras of the day. They couldn't have guessed what lay just around the corner with the explosion of pop music and for a year or two they were still a big attraction.

It was quite a shock to meet Harry Roy, which I did only once, one hot Saturday afternoon on the stage of a theatre in Camden Town which was for some years a BBC studio. It was mainly used for music, with or without audiences, and I believe some episodes of the Goon Show were also recorded there.

I had an image in mind of Harry Roy, quite unreasonably of course, that was founded on a photograph of him in a copy of *Picture Goer* that I had had as a boy. There he was, young and handsome, with curly dark hair, immaculately dressed in white tie and tails. The caption, I recall, described him as 'our own little hotchamacotcha Harry Roy'. I had also started to collect records by trying to buy at least one by every band going, and my Harry Roy example was a thoroughly disrespectful version of the quartet from *Rigoletto* which was called 'Swinging with Rig'. I loved it.

So, I turned up at the Camden Theatre early looking forward to meeting one of my idols. He was late. A band of session musicians had gathered on stage to be the Harry Roy band for that day, and then he came in. Old, rather bloated and purple about the face, not at all smartly dressed and wearing one of those diminutive trilby hats so often affected by stand-up comedians of the day. Harry's only words were, 'Blimey, it's hot.' And without more ado he stripped off down to a pair of combinations and, keeping his outrageous little hat on his head, conducted the broadcast thus attired.

Another band leader I had long admired and one who remained smart and well dressed to the end of his days was Geraldo, or Gerald Bright, to give him his real name. As a schoolboy in Coventry I would sometimes gather with a few like-minded wastrels in an alleyway behind Owen's Ballroom and there, with our ears pressed against the back wall of the building, we could just about hear the music, especially when Leslie 'Jiver' Hutchinson was lead trumpet. Leslie, by the way, was to become the father of that sophisticated and stylish singer, Elaine Delmar.

I did not often get to announce Geraldo's programmes, for in spite of his rather crude manner of speech he often did his own presentation. Older readers may remember the way in which he closed his programmes, saying, 'The clock on the wall says, Geraldo – it's time to go.' However, I was to be given a wonderful job eventually, travelling to New York and back with Geraldo and his orchestra aboard the legendary Queen Mary, recording material for thirteen hour-long programmes as we went. But that comes a little later in the story.

The bandleader with whom I became most closely acquainted and who was tremendously generous to me was Yorkshire-born Ken Mackintosh who, had he not taken on the onus of running a band on tour, might well have become one of the best jazz alto saxophone players Britain ever produced. We met on a long-running series of programmes of which the keynote was nostalgia. The band played big band hits of earlier years and I provided introductions of the 'do you remember when' variety. Ken and I hit it off right away, and he invited me to be his guest for a month in the Isle of Man where he regularly played a summer season in the Villa Marina. He rented a house for Pamela and myself, with Christopher, and all I had to do in return was to act as comedian-compère for Sunday night concerts. I introduced the band numbers, did a ten-minute stand-up spot of my own, and then announced the top-of-the-bill star who would be someone like Kenneth McKellar, or that lovely comedian Harry Worth. It was a superb experience and Ken thought I should have pursued a career as a comic, but I'm very glad that I didn't try. I was shortly to meet some of the most brilliant of that breed and I have to say that singularly few of them seemed to be happy men.

Ken never had any aspirations to do his own presentation on air, but of course he had to do it when touring ballrooms. I'm afraid his style became the butt of many a joke among his musicians. He would have been the first, I have no doubt, to admit his own short-comings in that area, and at least the jokes against him always had the ring of affection about them. In any case he had the last laugh himself because he ran a successful band for many years, he had hit records, and he had the satisfaction of seeing his daughter become one of the most sought-after session singers, and his son Andy an outstanding drummer and sax player.

Another short series of just four programmes led to, I think I can safely say, a mutual admiration society of three: myself, John Dankworth and Cleo Laine. John had sold to Jim Davidson, the head of popular music, the idea of putting together a huge band, some twenty-seven strong, from the cream of British jazz musicians; this included several bands within the band. Thus the brilliant trombonist Laurie Monk fronted a quintet, tenor sax player Danny Moss a quartet, and trumpet player Dickie Hawdon a larger group.

The singers were Tony Mansell, later to become a member of a fine harmony group called the Polka Dots, based on the American group the Hi-Los, and of course the incomparable Cleo Laine who is also Mrs Dankworth and these days the mother of an actress-singer daughter and a bass-player son. Almost the last time I met her she was dazzling audiences on Broadway as Mrs Puffer in a musical adaptation of *Edwin Drood*.

These programmes were produced by a man named John Burnaby, who was the son of a famous revue star of the twenties, Davey Burnaby. His knowledge of music of all kinds was vast and a feature of the programmes that he especially liked was that John would write a piece each week to feature a soloist from the ranks of outstanding classical musicians. The one I remember especially was the harpist Marie Goossens, sister of the world-famous oboist, Leon Goossens.

All I had to do on these occasions was to read a script that had been written by someone else, but the programmes were wonder-fully received and I have enjoyed the respect ever since not only of John and Cleo, but also of many of the musicians who made up that great band.

This period with the Light Programme also gave me the opportunity of introducing several record programmes. These were then the responsibility of the Gramophone Department, headed by a lady named Anna Instone, who chain-smoked and, under stress, stuttered somewhat. Her husband, Julian Herbage, introduced the long-running classical programme 'Music Magazine' that Anna produced, and he also for years ran the Promenade Concerts.

Most programmes, such as 'Housewives' Choice', were presented by outside freelance broadcasters, though I did get a couple of goes at that. It's worth mentioning as an example of the way things have changed, that Anna used to insist on a full script being submitted in advance and then on a full rehearsal of every day's programme, with the records played in full even though the producer knew in most cases exactly how long they lasted. This was real belt and braces stuff, of course; today the whole thing would be much more casual, with just a quick check of levels on the discs, a running order rather than a script, and links for the most part ad-libbed. And in my opinion that has led in most cases to a much better style of presentation.

The sort of programmes that were more likely to come my way as a staff announcer were such things as 'Three Band Session' which I did with my old friend Jack Dabbs – he had given me my first ever BBC jazz programme several years earlier, when I was a milkman. The title speaks for itself, but we would make up programmes with American bands, big and small, that were still just names to most British fans.

In between these more glamorous jobs there were long, comparatively boring periods spent in the confines of continuity. For three or four hours at a stretch I would sit and listen to other people's programme output, filling in the gaps by trailing programmes still to come and generally dealing with little day to day dilemmas such as discovering that a recorded programme listed on the schedule as lasting for, say, twenty-nine and a half minutes suddenly ran out of steam at twenty-six and a half. This is still very much what happens in a network continuity suite today but there is one basic difference. In the days I'm recalling we always had a standby record on the turntable and, having checked its duration to the second, we could start it spinning at exactly the second that would fill the time up to the next programme junction. Then, if the programme on air should under-run, all we had to do was fade up the record. You might still hear this technique used at the end of an hour of the Jimmy Young show when Jim hasn't quite worked his timing out neatly, but in that case the chances are, as I've seen for myself, an assistant has crept in unobtrusively and crouching down below the desk has set up the disc in readiness for him.

Personally I used to enjoy most of the programmes going by during a continuity shift and I also took pleasure in trying to find possible fill records that were at least appropriate in the event of a tape running short. There were others who, after many more years than I had spent in the business, had no interest in what was going on at all. One chap in particular, as soon as he was installed at the beginning of his shift, switched his desk into what is termed rehearsal condition, which means that his loudspeakers were cut; he would then swing his feet up on to the desk and bury himself in a book or newspaper, relying on the engineer in an adjoining cubicle to warn him if anything was going wrong. As you can imagine, if he was suddenly jerked to attention the manner in which he dealt with a hiatus sounded pretty ghastly.

This boredom stemming from over familiarity would sometimes reach into the engineer's compartment as well; among my favourite stories is one concerning an attempt by one man to liven up his day.

Part of the responsibility on that side of the glass, entirely out of the announcer's hands, was to fade up a channel putting the Greenwich Time Signal, the famous six pips, on air. An occasional fault was for an engineer, due to a slight lapse of attention, to clip the first pip or, due to excess zeal perhaps, to cut off the last one. This would immediately prompt a call from the head man in the control room seeking an explanation.

[115]

The man in my story was on duty one deadly early morning shift; he had a young trainee beside him and decided to demonstrate his dexterity with an amusing but unwise ploy. By unauthorised cross-plugging of his jack field he fed the pips channel through to not one but two separate faders. His plan was to fade up the first pip with his left hand then, closing that fader, to open another with his right hand and so on, alternately for the five seconds the six pips lasted. This, he told the trainee who is now an accomplished and experienced producer, was a great way of staying awake and alert.

Unfortunately when the great moment arrived he wasn't quite as slick as he intended, so that the sequence as heard in the cubicle ran something like: Pip, (silence), pip, pip, (silence), pip.

Knowing that retribution was nigh he then rang control room to own up and said, 'I'm sorry, I'm afraid I crashed the pips.' 'Oh yes,' came the yawned response at the other end, 'which one, the first or the last?'

'You're not going to believe this,' continued the penitent engineer, 'but it was actually the second and the fifth.'

One other aspect of the Light Programme announcer's routine, much sought after by some of us, was to be the regular man on a comedy series. If you were lucky this meant that in addition to speaking the opening words and reading the closing credits you might also be given a couple of lines in one of the sketches. Some of my colleagues made quite a name for themselves in this direction: there was Wallace Greenslade with the Goons, David Dunhill, known as Dunners, in 'Take it From Here', and Ronnie Fletcher in some of the Kenneth Horne series.

The attraction no doubt lay in rubbing shoulders with famous comedians, in deluding oneself that one was also a performer of sorts, and in exchanging temporarily the solitary life of the continuity announcer for the gregarious atmosphere of stage and audience.

Quite early on in my career I was asked to take on the residency in 'Take It From Here', written by Frank Muir and Denis Norden, starring Jimmy Edwards, Dick Bentley and June Whitfield with the now long defunct BBC Revue Orchestra, conducted by Harry Rabinowitz.

This elevation to the announcers' peerage occurred during my extremely impecunious days but Pamela decided this wasn't going to show itself if we could help it. We therefore went along to Simpsons in Piccadilly and bought me not only a suit we could ill afford, but also a shirt and matching tie for my stage debut among the illustrious.

The programme was recorded in the Paris studio in Lower Regent Street which is still used for comedy and quiz shows that need an audience. At some stage in its history it had been a cinema and, as it is situated deep in a basement, it was also utilised during the early years of World War Two as an air raid shelter. Rumour has it that one night when it was filling this function a bomb actually landed right down the air shaft from the roof of this building, coming to rest just above the studio and fortunately failing to explode. This may well be apochryphal, as I heard it told on many occasions by producers doing warm-ups for their shows. They invariably ended by saying, 'And as far as I know, it's still there!' The warm-up is, of course, a jolly little period of varying length during which a producer will introduce his cast to the studio audience and the cast will then try to get the said audience laughing inordinately before the broadcast begins.

On the occasion of my 'Take It From Here' debut, producer Charles Maxwell introduced two gangling fops, Frank Muir and Denis Norden; they did a little double-act of their own before bringing on Jimmy and Dick who then, as I was to learn, went through precisely the same routine week after week.

Jimmy invariably brought on stage one of the instruments he played, after a fashion, sometimes his trombone or euphonium, but usually a trumpet. Then after a few gags he would offer to play a request, feigning to hear someone in the audience ask for 'Flight of the Bumblebee' which was extremely popular at the time, thanks to a dazzling recording by Harry James. Jimmy would pause just long enough for us all to think that he really was going to play it and, raising the trumpet almost to his lips, he would then blow a tremendous raspberry across the front of the mike, adding, 'That was the bumblebee in a hurry to get to his honey.' Another pause. Then another raspberry, moving his head in the opposite direction, 'And that was the same bumblebee going home again.' It never failed.

Dick Bentley, who was Australian, always told a story to the effect that during the past week he had been introduced to the British sport of hunting. 'And Jimmy,' he would say, 'a bigger load of red-faced, pot-bellied, moustachioed . . . (nicely gauged pause for giggles) . . . and the men were just as bad.' Big laugh.

Having gone through the routine, Frank and Denis on this occasion returned to the stage to introduce me as it was my first time on the show. A few kind words, ending with '. . . and here he is. Brian Matthew. . .'

I stepped, blushing, before the audience. But Frank had not finished. Casting a sidelong glance in my direction, he drawled, '. . . a symphony in beige.'

During my spell with this historic comedy show I never had many extra lines written in for me, but we did go on one occasion to record the show at a Royal Naval base near Portsmouth and Jimmy decided to roughen up his warm-up act a little in a routine which required the quaffing in a single breath of pints of bitter. He asked me to be his stooge and straight man for this little act, bringing on the pints and delivering his feed lines. A thrilling experience for me.

When the series finally ran its course, Jimmy generously hosted a dinner party in an exclusive Chelsea club to which he invited all members of staff with their spouses. I never met anyone else who made such a gesture on so grand a scale. Jimmy's humour was of a style that has always appealed to me. He was a cultured and educated man. Indeed he had been a school master at one time. Yet his forte was for the brash and vulgar and he never baulked at shocking an audience into laughter. Whatever it says about me, I have to confess that I liked his approach. I regretted Jimmy's final decision to withdraw to some extent from the business to concentrate on farming and indulge his passion for riding.

The next comedy show that I was, to say the least, overawed to join for a couple of years was 'Hancock's Half Hour' with its brilliant central clown and unique style that has never, in my view, been surpassed. A great comedy show is never, as Tony was to discover to his cost, the work of one person alone and the great strengths of this one were its supporting cast and the wonderful made-to-measure scripts by Ray Galton and Alan Simpson.

I became almost immediately aware of the paranoid personality that dogged Tony Hancock throughout his career. He would turn up at the theatre week after week in a dour, uncommunicative mood, demand to see the script and then sit alone in the stalls, still clad in homburg and overcoat, reading and from time to time muttering, 'This isn't funny. I can't make that work. I'll never get a laugh out of that.'

I could never understand this because I had always read the script myself in advance, hearing in my head just what Tony could and would do with the lines. When I first experienced this, however, I was amazed that no one seemed even remotely put out and that no attempt was made to change a word that had been written. Wisely, of course, since they had all heard it before. Then came the recording and those wonderful jokes were brought miraculously to life as Ray and Alan had known perfectly well they would be.

Tony was also a loner who never socialised with his supporting cast, so far as I could see, conversing only with his manager, a lady named Freddie whom he eventually married. Yet what lovely, friendly people he had around him in Hattie Jacques, Bill Kerr, Sid James and, eccentric though he may have been, that comic genius Kenneth Williams.

The warm-up was as much a tradition with this show as with any other, but it must have been unique in so far as the star of the show never took part in it. All the jokes came from the writers and from Bill and Sid, with Kenneth perhaps contributing some of his repertoire of funny voices.

For a short period, and for reasons long since lost in the mist of time, we left our normal studio and recorded the Hancock programmes on the stage of the tiny four hundred and thirty seater Fortune Theatre in Russell Street, opposite the colonnades of the huge Theatre Royal, Drury Lane. This bijou theatre housed during the week a play that, whatever it was, featured a substantial tree set centre stage. This was no real problem as 'Hancock's Half Hour' was played on the apron before the front cloth and as Ray and Alan introduced the cast the actors made their entrances between the velvet drapes. One night, Kenneth was chatting to me in the wings, telling outrageous jokes, when he suddenly heard his introduction, swept centre stage, collided with the tree and bellowed, 'Oh, fuck!' and then stuck his head, bleeding from the forehead, through the drapes and uttered that well-known inane 'Ulloh'.

I remember, too, an embarrassing week in this same theatre when there was a technical break-down in the middle of the recording which took a very long time to sort out; we were anxious for the audience not to leave before we had finished. Despite blandishments and cajoling from the rest of the cast Tony flatly refused to make any contribution, leaving the impromptu routines mainly to Ray and Alan. It was at that moment I realised that the genius of Hancock could only thrive with a script. He was in fact an actor who could not exist divorced from his role; he was quite incapable of ad-libbing, for he had no fund of jokes like Ted Ray or to a lesser extent Tommy Trinder, both of whom were never at a loss for words.

Another great failing of Hancock's, which manifested itself long before he reached the end of his tragic road, was that he didn't trust his fellow actors. He felt they were somehow trying to steal his limelight and so he insisted on having them, one by one, removed from the cast of his show. From this it was a short step to deluding himself that he didn't need anyone else. He wrote, directed and starred in a film called *The Punch and Judy Man* which was so awful that it never got a London showing, dribbled out on release, and sank without trace. I've never been able to find anyone who admits to having seen it. Yet I have to admit to playing a minute unseen part in its making. Tony rang me and asked if I would go out to Elstree and record a few lines. There was, it seems, a sequence in which he was seen waking up and switching on a radio and he wanted me to be the presenter of that programme. I happily went out to the famous studios and was directed to a sound stage; there was Tony, quite alone, with a script on a lectern. He swept forward in what was to me an unfamiliar 'actor laddie' manner, threw out his hand and in an entirely uncharacteristic 'posh' voice thanked me for coming. I still cringe at the memory of that bizarre moment, for it showed him to me as the true example of the flawed genius. I should prefer to remember him for the many weeks during which I was able to watch him at first hand lifting gems from the printed page and delivering them with unmatched timing.

I was by this time approaching another of my crossroads, though I could scarcely have guessed that this one would have such far-reaching effects on my career and life-style. A producer named Jimmy Grant, with whom I had worked from time to time, devised a programme quite unlike anything that had been heard on BBC radio before. It was very much by way of an experiment and he asked me if I would like to introduce it. It was called 'Saturday Skiffle Club'.

[16]

'Skiffle' is a marvellous word. Its origins are obscure, but the music has its roots in folk and jazz and is performed, generally, on guitars and unorthodox instruments – the tea-chest bass, the washboard and the jug. The word 'skiffle' seems to have an onomatopoeic quality somehow redolent of the music itself.

In the mid to late fifties British bandleader Chris Barber encouraged the formation within his band of a smaller skiffle group led by his banjo player Lonnie Donegan; they would regularly play a set during gigs. Lonnie soon became so popular for this side of his work that he left Chris's band and went on the road in his own right. Even more significantly, he had almost single-handedly started what was soon to be a nation-wide craze among young people. The attractions of this sort of music were obvious; it was bright and jolly and best of all it was of the do-it-yourself variety that bypassed the expense of buying conventional instruments.

BBC producer Jimmy Grant, who specialised in jazz pro-grammes and was himself an accomplished pianist (he played in semi-pro dance and jazz bands), very soon recognised the growing popularity and the scope for the further expansion of skiffle. His suggestion of a weekly half-hour programme was taken up and he was given thirty minutes at ten o'clock on Saturday mornings, a spot hitherto occupied by cinema organists. He asked me if I would like to introduce the shows and although at that stage I hadn't a clue what skiffle might be I liked the idea and jumped at the opportunity.

'Skiffle Club' was an instant success and immediately started to attract a large young audience. New groups and bands sprouted up

THE MESSAGE IN THIS
CARD READS:-

HOPE YOUR DAY
IS VERY SPECIAL
AND THEN WHEN IT IS THROUGH,
THE FUTURE WILL BRING EVERYTHING
THAT MEANS THE MOST TO YOU.

CONGRATULATIONS ON
YOUR 21ST BIRTHDAY

KC2590

£5 OFF
VIDEO CAMERA HIRE
WHEN YOU PRESENT THIS VOUCHER

Why not capture that special
celebration and keep those
memories forever. You can
even make your own
movies by renting a video
camera from Radio Rentals.

PLEASE COMPLETE (BLOCK CAPITALS)
AND PRESENT AT YOUR NEAREST RADIO RENTALS SHOP.

Mr/Mrs/Miss _____

Address _____

Town _____ County _____

Postcode _____ Tel No (Daytime) _____

Tel No (Evening) _____ Signature _____

I currently rent from Radio Rentals   YES ☐   NO ☐

Check the Yellow Pages for your nearest showroom

*radio*RENTALS.

overnight and we never had any problem finding enough enthusiasts to fill the bill. The names of the groups were weird and wonderful; one that I remember particularly was Russell Quay's 'City Ramblers'. Russell himself occasionally indulged in a spot of jug blowing, using a stone pitcher; by blowing across its mouth he produced deep bass notes. There was also a young man who had made himself an instrument by wedging a broom handle into the corner of a tea chest; he then attached a string from the top of the handle to the opposite corner of the box. By flexing the handle and plucking the string it was possible to play several different bass notes. Tea-chest basses were quite common, but this particular exponent went on to make himself a proper four-stringed instrument, then acquired a real bass and eventually became an extremely accomplished full-time professional musician.

Another regular team to appear on 'Skiffle Club' was the Chas McDevitt Skiffle Group who had a sizeable hit record called 'Freight Train' featuring the voice of Nancy Whiskey. When she left the group Chas replaced her with another girl whom he subsequently married, then when the skiffle craze began to cool down they opened a coffee bar in Berwick Street in Soho. Sadly, it isn't there any more and I haven't heard of them from that day to this.

As the programme developed over a couple of years Jimmy started to diversify from the original concept and introduced more folky elements, Jim Hall and Robin McGregor among them, while many of the groups began to introduce more sophisticated instruments, electric guitars for instance. Skiffle was on its way out and rock and roll on its way in.

Delighted with the unexpectedly big success of this experimental half hour the head of the department, Jim Davidson, then asked Jimmy if he could come up with a formula to fill two hours on Saturday mornings. He did so and a programme was born that was destined to run for ten years, certainly the first and far and away the most important breakthrough for pop music on British radio. It was called 'Saturday Club'.

[123]

In those days, due to a tripartite agreement between the BBC, the record companies and the Musicians' Union, there was a strictly observed restriction called needle time which limited the total length of time during which gramophone records could be broadcast. Our ration on 'Saturday Club' was something like twenty-eight minutes, so three-quarters of the show had to consist of sessions which we recorded during the week; one group would appear live with me in the studio on Saturday mornings.

We would play six or seven request records each week and three 'new to you' discs chosen from current releases, feature a trad jazz band in the 'jazz cellar' and introduce some of the emergent young groups cheek by jowl with long-established soloists and harmony groups from the previous decade.

Jimmy himself composed a signature tune called 'Saturday Jump'; as recorded by Humphrey Lyttleton's band this introduced the programme for years. Recently on a live show with Humph in Blackpool I asked him if he could remember that tune and he said: 'Not a note of it.' He confessed to me after the performance that he'd been scared stiff I was going to ask him to play it!

Shortly after 'Saturday Club' got going many American stars began to appear in Britain; although they were allowed to perform live on stage they were not allowed, for a while, to broadcast. They could and did visit my studio for short interviews to promote their records and it was in this way that I first met Bobby Darin, Della Reese, Sammy Davis and many other artists. This became a very popular aspect of the show; it was even better when in due course we were permitted to record sessions with them. Then we were able to feature Bobby Vee, Gene Vincent, Diana Ross and the Supremes, Martha and the Vandellas, and the Everly Brothers, to name but a few.

One of the studios we used for our sessions was in Piccadilly and it was a small theatre, with a low stage and a few rows of seats. The control cubicle was up at the back where a circle would have been and alongside it was the recording booth that gave on to a tiny balcony over the auditorium. On one momentous occasion we had booked a double session with two seminal figures of rock and roll, both alas no longer with us, Gene Vincent and Eddie Cochran. Gene, who was lame, recorded his songs first and was limping to the back of the theatre when Eddie, about to start his set, called out, 'C'm'ere Vincent. You aint goin' no place, I got yer crutches. C'mon up on stage and jam with me.'

Gene went back to the stage, got out his guitar again, and for fifteen or twenty minutes these legendary characters swapped choruses and sang duets. When it was all over, Vincent packed up again and left the studio, at which point the recording engineer appeared on the small balcony and said rather wistfully, 'Was I supposed to record that?' A unique occasion had gone and the opportunity of a priceless addition to BBC archives was lost. Gene and Eddie never did record together, ever; furthermore, a few months later, they were in a car crash which resulted in Eddie's death.

Another venue we used regularly was the Playhouse Theatre on the Embankment in London, and there we were scheduled to record a set with the Everly Brothers on the very day that they arrived in the country. The time of the session came, but Don and Phil didn't, and as the minutes rolled by we began to get more and more anxious. Our time was limited, because the studio was booked for something else after us and there was no chance of going beyond our allotted span. Eventually panic phone calls revealed that their plane had indeed landed and they were somewhere on their way to us. When they finally arrived, we had less than half an hour of our original three hours left, but the boys got straight on stage, gave one brief example of a level into the microphones which of course had long been in place, and then within the space of eighteen minutes they performed six of their famous songs, flawlessly. It was one of the most extraordinary sessions I ever attended in a studio.

Compared with the effects that are commonplace in recording today, we were severely limited in the late fifties and into the sixties, and the BBC lagged behind commercial studios in terms of the equipment at our disposal, though not in terms of sound and recording engineers, of whom we had the very best. One such unsung hero was an eccentric genius named Freddie Harris who overcame most of the problems presented to him and went about his business in a way that was all his own. As a producer, one needed to have total confidence in Fred, for while you sat frustrated in the control box desperate to hear something, he would be wandering round the studio, in amongst the musicians, adjusting microphones and listening live to the sounds he knew he was going to capture.

Most of our mikes were live on both sides and Fred was the first person I saw block off one side with a cigarette packet which he attached with an elastic band, thus blocking out sounds that would otherwise have spilled over from instruments where he didn't want them. He also spent hours at home making up his own special double-end cords which had the effect of limiters, long before such refinements had been introduced.

Fred had one pace of working. His own. He was a quietly spoken man of few words who could drive you mad with frustration as he mulled over a problem, silently, while rolling a fag, but he always came up with the goods in time. I believe he was equally frustrating at home where he had dismantled his old car, leaving parts of the engine strewn in their oiliness all over the kitchen table until his wife threatened retribution with a carving knife.

On another occasion he had balanced a rehearsal with the Oscar Rabin band and in the break before transmission Fred retired to a toilet, high in the building, where he succeeded in locking himself in. The producer was going out of his mind as the 'on air' time approached until he received a message that Fred had been seen emerging from a window and climbing, spider-like, down the outside of the edifice. Happily he arrived on time as usual. They don't make them like Fred Harris any more, but many younger men learned all they knew from him and never ceased to be grateful for their good fortune in having him as a colleague.

As the years went by and before the advent of the pirate radio stations, 'Saturday Club' went from strength to strength and all the big names in the pop business were lining up to appear on the show.

[126]

The Beatles performed live one Saturday morning, when their fame had spread a little beyond Liverpool and Hamburg, and I first met Brian Epstein, who was to become a personal friend and a colleague in a venture we almost got off the ground. We were planning to build a new theatre, but this was scotched to some extent by Brian's untimely death.

Our listening audience grew beyond everyone's wildest expectations so that at our peak we had as many as twenty million tuned to us between ten o'clock and noon on Saturdays. Our post bag was phenomenal and we were far and away the most successful popular music show there had ever been.

There was one funny little sour note to all this, which stemmed from my conscious attempt to get away from staid, formal BBC speech delivery and to adopt a rather more plebeian approach.

Every week, when we came off the air, the four or five of us responsible for the transmission would repair over the road to the BBC Club on the ground floor of the building which has now newly risen again as the famous Edwardian Langham Hotel; there we would relax over a beer or two. One day, at the height of our fame, my old senior announcer Frank Phillips weaved his way towards me as I was getting a round of drinks. He had obviously already been there a lot longer than I had and as he glared belligerently into my eyes he said, 'I'd like to punch you on the bloody jaw.' 'Whatever for, Frank?' I asked, more than a touch flabbergasted by his manner. 'For what you're doing to the English language,' he snapped.

He was probably justified, I suppose, but I wonder however he would react nowadays to, say, Derek Jameson.

Such venom, however, was rare. We were much more accustomed to receiving eulogies for what we had achieved. There were, too, spin-offs in the form of all-star concerts that played to capacity in the Royal Albert Hall; I have in my memorabilia a programme for one such called 'Saturday Club Jazz and Rock Night' with a bill that included the bands of Acker Bilk, Terry Lightfoot and John Barry; the soloists were Adam Faith, Clinton Ford, Craig Douglas,

The Lana Sisters, The Dallas Boys, George Chisholm and Bert Weedon, among others.

On another of these mammoth galas I was to be co-presenter with a freelance named Denny Piercey who had in the past been a drummer, I believe. Adam Faith was scheduled to appear on this one as well, together with Cliff Richard and the Shadows and just about everyone who was anyone in British pop music. At rehearsal Adam's manager, a tough old harridan named Eve Taylor, let it be known that unless Adam's fee was raised to a thousand pounds he would not go on. I should point out that not many people would get a radio fee like that today; in those days it was quite unheard of.

Our boss Jim Davidson sat on one side of the hall, glowering, and Evie perched herself, intractible, on the other. I was designated the go-between and trotted back and forth with attempts at negotiation. Arguments that Adam would have been conspicuous by his absence from such an illustrious bill cut no ice.

Then Jim played his master card. 'Look, Brian,' he said, 'go back to Evie and tell her I remember her when she was on the halls herself, singing "Rule Britannia" while she lifted her skirts up showing Union Jack knickers and banging cymbals together with her knees. And Adam gets the same money as everybody else.'

I don't think I quite relayed the message verbatim, but whatever I retained from the original bore fruit and Adam duly sang. Not without one other hiccup, though. Jim thought it would be an impressive idea for Adam to go on in darkness and to shine a torch on girls in the audience as he sang 'Poor Me'.

This must have appealed to Eve Taylor's old showbiz instincts because she readily agreed to the idea. It was my first exposure to teenybop hysteria, though nothing on the scale that I was to witness later in the States with the Beatles, but still frightening enough for the performers. Denny Piercey and I had to take stations either side of Adam on stage and throw shrieking, weeping girls back into the auditorium as they tried to scale the stage.

I also saw an amazing display of courage from my old friend Clinton Ford. He had had considerable success with his recording of a maudlin old favourite from the Elvis Presley repertoire about a boy and his dog, Old Shep. I had persuaded Clint, against his better judgement, to sing it on stage at the Royal Albert Hall. He had scarcely got halfway through the song when he was drowned out by yells of: 'We want Elvis.' It was terrifying and awful, and my fault. But Clint stood his ground and waited. As the cacophony abated somewhat he said in his best Kentucky drawl: 'Ah'm gonna finish this song if it kills me.' There was a moment's silence then the huge auditorium erupted with cheers and applause. Clint duly finished the song and stopped the show. I should have remembered that a British crowd will nearly always support the underdog in the end.

After a few years BBC management decided that Jimmy Grant and I should be rewarded for our efforts and what a present they dreamed up for us. A regular programme of the time with Geraldo and his Orchestra was called 'Tip Top Tunes' and one of Geraldo's businesses away from the BBC entailed supplying bands for Cunard cruise ships; they were known as Geraldo's navy. So, what an idea, someone thought, to have Gerry himself front a large specially recruited band for the New York round trip on board the *Queen Mary*. Then we could record enough material during the ten days of performances to make, with interviews with celebrities and crew, thirteen programmes called 'Tip Top Crossing'.

When I got home and gave the news to Pamela she said, 'Well, you're not going without me!' This message, duly relayed to management, caused a few raised eyebrows, but I was told that she could go if we paid her fare ourselves. We were to travel first class, but the Cunard publicity officer said he could fix it for me if I would agree to pay the tourist class rate. Even this was beyond our means in those days, but a wise old friend suggested we should consult our bank manager and to our utter astonishment he said it was an opportunity not to be missed and agreed to arrange a loan. Pamela then visited all her friends borrowing evening dresses, and we set off for ten days of the most pampered luxury that the civilised world had to offer.

As well as compèring all the first class lounge concerts which were to form the basis of our broadcasts I also had to cover every inch of the ship, from the depths of the engine room to the swaying crow's nest, to record short interviews reflecting life on board. There was, however, one area that was strictly taboo to all passengers and that was the crew's off-duty pub known as 'The Pig and Whistle', below decks in the stern of this mighty vessel. However, among the passengers on this outward voyage to New York were Gracie Fields and her Italian husband, Boris. Our Gracie agreed to give an impromptu concert for the lads and, provided we didn't attempt to make any recordings, it was agreed that we should also be allowed to attend this unusual event. The Lancashire lass sang her heart out and it was a privilege to be present.

Our party for this trip consisted of Jimmy Grant, myself and Pamela, singers Rosemary Squires and Don Rennie, a BBC engineer and a sound effects man whose careers had also singled them out for commendation. We were a happy crowd and every mealtime was a mirthful, and I'm afraid noisy, celebration. At the adjoining table, in solitary state sat an elderly bishop, purple of hue and solemn of bearing. On finally arriving in New York I felt bound to make apologies for the disturbance we caused. To my delight, he introduced himself as the Bishop of New Jersey and said it did him some good to see people enjoying themselves so much; he only wished he could have joined us.

Every morning I used to attend the purser's cocktail party, meeting the passengers specially chosen for this privilege and fixing up quite a few interviews as a result; he also gave me the state room phone numbers of others who chose not to attend. These included Victor Mature. Victor had booked three adjoining state rooms, one for himself, one for his female companion, and one in the middle for his hi-fi equipment so that he could play music without disturbing his neighbours. At length I plucked up courage to ring him and a sleepy voice mumbled in my receiver. He then repeated what I had said to a companion and came back to me. It was very obvious that he was in bed and equally obvious that he was not alone. Anyway,

[130]

he made an appointment to meet me, but unfortunately he failed to keep the assignation.

I'm afraid that gave extra relish for me to the story I was told by the athlete who ran the ship's gymnasium for passengers trying to lose the excess avoirdupois gained in the dining room. It seems that Mature turned up with his girl friend and to impress her picked up the diminutive athlete, hoisting him across his shoulders in the all-in wrestlers' aeroplane spin. 'Get out of that, yer bum,' growled Mature. The athlete promptly obliged and once on his feet sent the giant film star sprawling. 'Serves you right, you bastard,' said his lady love.

As we were only going to be in New York for twenty-four hours for the turn round of the *Queen Mary*, I had made arrangements with a record company in London to make sure our day was as incident packed as possible. So, on arrival at our hotel, we were whisked away in a limousine to do the mandatory tourist things; a visit to the top of the Empire State Building was one of them. Then we were taken to the recording studios and home of Pat Boone who, at that time, was one of the brightest young stars in American music. He graciously allowed me to record a lengthy interview which provided me with a bonus extra programme on our return.

After being entertained to a sumptuous dinner where we tasted for the first time soft-shell crabs, a great delicacy, we were whisked off to a theatre to see the hit show *Gypsy* starring Ethel Merman. As an unexpected additional attraction we found ourselves sitting immediately behind the beautiful British actress Greer Garson, still looking for all the world as she had looked in *Mrs Miniver*.

As if that were not enough, after the show we were escorted to one of the most famous of jazz clubs, now long since vanished, Basin Street East. Among the seven or eight attractions appearing that night were a wonderful singer named Chris Connor and a great band, the Herbie Mann Octet.

We got back to our hotel late, but in time to sample the novelty of multi-channel television; as we were due to sail at noon we rose early to go shopping for gifts, especially for little Christopher left at home in Coventry with his grandmother. Unfortunately no one had told us that in New York the big stores did not open until ten o'clock so we wandered around the streets frozen by a biting wind coming up from the East river, popping into coffee stalls when we couldn't bear it any longer, then diving into Macy's the moment they opened to buy whatever we could afford, and making it back to the ship in the nick of time.

I don't know whether Chris remembers those New York presents. I do. There was a battery-operated dog that walked about and barked, and a wind-up car that would collide with wall or chair and fall into several pieces. It was quite wonderful and I should like to have one now.

Before the *Queen Mary* cast off from a New York pier for the return voyage there was a cocktail party given by Cunard's publicity man, Douglas Lobley. The BBC team was invited and we reached a high level of good cheer by the time we sailed. Pamela and I had had the temerity to say that our state room was not as pleasant as the one on the way out, and as there were fewer passengers making the return Douglas insisted on sending us with an assistant purser to choose another cabin. In our euphoric condition we were willing to accept the first one we came to, but the young guide had obviously been instructed by Douglas to make sure that we should be shown everything available. It took a very long time and was an effective way of putting us in our place.

A thrilling highlight occurred in mid Atlantic when we were due to pass, at close quarters, the *Queen Elizabeth* going in the opposite direction. The captain informed all passengers and the decks were thronged with cheering people as the two greatest passenger liners in the world came within hailing distance of each other some fifteen hundred miles from the nearest land.

I imagine there are not many people alive today who can say they made the two-way Atlantic crossing aboard that beautiful ship the *Queen Mary*, and it was certainly an experience that we have always treasured. In fact we still have the full set of lunch and dinner menus; they were different for every meal. The *Queen Mary*'s dining room also boasted that they could provide any dish that a passenger might desire even though it was not on the menu. We briefly played the game of trying to catch them out with such diverse suggestions as tripe and onions, or larks' tongues in aspic, but we failed to disconcert them a jot.

Not long after our return to England I decided that I had had enough of being an announcer and asked if I could transfer to Aeolian Hall as a producer. Chief announcer John Snagge was very sympathetic and agreed that it would probably be a good career move. Jim Davidson of Light Entertainment was also willing to take me on for a trial period, provided I agreed to continue introducing 'Saturday Club'. He was a great believer, he always claimed, in not interfering with a winning team. For example he did not personally like the Billy Cotton Band Show on Sunday lunch times, he told me, but nothing in the world would persuade him to take it off.

So I moved into a small office on the top floor of Aeolian Hall, now the property of Sotheby's. The young lady sent to me as a secretary was a rather serious teenager named Frances Line; she is now the controller of Radio Two.

Not long after I had settled in, Jim Davidson said that now we had got Saturday morning sewn up he would like to turn his attention to Sundays. Could I, he wondered, dream up a concept aimed at the same audience but one hour in length, and with a live audience show as well? After some trial and error, and a pilot show with Jim's own title, 'Rumpus Room', we finally settled on a format for a programme that was eventually known as 'Easy Beat' and was recorded on Wednesday evenings in the Playhouse Theatre.

The plan was to have a resident band which would play its own numbers and accompany guest soloists, a guest jazz band and either a folk or rock group. We also featured a teenage panel in a sort of 'Juke Box Jury' spot in which they gave thumbs up or down to new releases. Funnily enough I still occasionally get letters today from people who appeared in that capacity as youngsters.

Our original resident band was the John Barry Seven, and what a

[133]

talented group they were. John himself, of course, has long established a reputation as an outstanding composer of film scores, especially for the James Bond movies; in my view perhaps his best work ever was the music he wrote for *The Lion in Winter*. Then on piano there was Les Reed, who was soon to emerge as a very successful songwriter; the guitarist was Vic Flick, who has long been one of the most sought-after session musicians in the business, while the drummer was Dougie Wright whom I was to meet often in later years when I was producing records.

The first trad band we employed was Kenny Ball's Jazzmen, nicely timed to coincide with Kenny's hit recordings of 'Samantha' and 'Midnight in Moscow', while an early guest singer was Frank Ifield. I asked a record company A & R man if he could recommend a young unknown girl singer, and that was how we found Maureen Evans, who stayed with the show for a long time.

Once again it seemed we had hit on a successful formula and again the listening figures, which measured the estimated size of audience, rose dramatically. This time there was the added attraction that we also gained a cult following at the theatre and week after week the Playhouse was packed to capacity.

My life was fascinating from my own point of view and I also thought that I was fully occupied, but once again big changes were just around the corner and we'll get to them after I've taken a little time to explain what was happening in my private life away from the BBC.

[17]

When we first came to live in Chelsfield in Kent I was kept more than busy at the BBC, but Pamela desperately needed an interest outside the home to avoid the boredom of semi-isolation. When she spotted an item in the local paper indicating that the village dramatic society needed a producer she thought it might be the answer. So she borrowed a bicycle and rode to a meeting in the village hall, joined the society as an actress and volunteered me as producer!

Rehearsals were conducted mainly in our home to get round the problem of baby-sitters, and after some of the society members had got over the shock of being expected to work like professionals instead of simply doing it for fun we began to attract a lot of interest.

The first move was to step up output from two to four productions a year; these were to include, during summer, an open-air Shakespeare and at Christmas a pantomime which we wrote ourselves. Then we set out to find and encourage local youngsters with talents and interests in the staging of plays. In this area we were extremely lucky to find three teenagers who were between them to fulfil almost all our requirements. One was training to be an electronics engineer and had a natural aptitude for stage lighting which has lasted to this day. He not only designed and built a marvellous little lighting board for our own small private theatre, but now often directs the elaborate lighting from the large modern computer-controlled board at the Churchill Theatre in Bromley when it houses productions by amateur operatic societies.

Next we met a young lady about to go to art college with an expressed interest in costume design. She was to design and make costumes for us for many varied productions; some of these are still in use now. She herself went on to work professionally at the Marlowe Theatre in Canterbury and, now married and a mother, still does special projects.

Our third 'discovery' was a young man who wasn't too happy with his chosen profession. He was a promising young actor who also showed a flair for set design. He also told me confidentially that he would like to train to be an architect. With a little encouragement he applied and was accepted for training and has now for many years been a qualified architect who still takes an active interest in amateur theatre.

It didn't take me very long to discover that I wanted to play as well as direct so fairly soon Pamela and I were frequently performing coveted roles and mounting quite elaborate productions. For an open-air *Midsummer Night's Dream* in which we appeared as Oberon and Titania we recruited a fourteen-piece orchestra from the Guildhall and a troupe of fairies from a children's dancing school. There can seldom have been a Titania who had so much trouble keeping her minions in order, preventing them from climbing trees and standing on their heads in the woods. Though, come to think of it, if I were directing the play today I think I should encourage both activities.

During the time we spent with the Chelsfield Players we also moved to a larger house in the same district and eventually built an extension as a games room. Owing to the shape of the house this extension was a split-level room, dividing itself fortuitously into stage and auditorium areas; it was therefore ideal for rehearsals. Eventually, however, we fell out with the society and formed one of our own which we called the Pilgrim Players; we then set about equipping our small home theatre with adequate lighting and stereo sound.

At about this time, through broadcasts with the Beatles, I met Brian Epstein and learned of his keen interest in theatre. We soon set up a company with the purpose of building a theatre in a rural setting close to Orpington and Brian undertook to raise the money for the project. We recruited an architect who had specialised in this field and he came up with a design for a three hundred and fifty seater that incorporated a foyer which would also serve as an art gallery. I meanwhile had meetings with BBC management who were beginning to anticipate problems over studio accommodation for recorded sessions and an interest was expressed in renting the theatre during the daytime for these sessions; there would be ample parking available for musicians.

At the time Orpington had its own council and it didn't take long to persuade them of the desirability of having such an arts centre in their district with the result that they offered us an ideal site on a nearby country estate.

It all seemed too good to be true, and it was. Before long Orpington ceased to be autonomous and we were absorbed into the Greater London district of Bromley where there were already plans to build, at public expense, what is now the Churchill Theatre. Local councillors were not going to tolerate a situation in which private enterprise competed with their efforts. They rescinded the decision to make land available to us and someone launched a scurrilous campaign suggesting that, because of our known professional activities, Epstein and I were trying to set up a pop recording studio in a quiet rural area.

It was not very long after this episode that Brian Epstein died, and the theatre project with him. This failure was the source of deep regret at the time but when I see now the great difficulty with which any surviving little theatres are kept afloat I have to admit that I feel relieved not to have been saddled with that responsibility.

Our next move was to attempt to run our own tiny theatre at home on a club basis. We began to mount many more productions, using out of work professional friends whenever possible, and building up a sizeable mailing list of patrons. No charge was made for admission but voluntary subscriptions were requested which covered expenses and allowed us to make regular donations to a charity.

[137]

The response was remarkable and we soon had several hundred regular supporters. As a result our tiny close of five houses was regularly filled with cars. Almost everyone put up with the inconvenience without complaint. There were two exceptions, however, with council connections and they manoeuvred an order for us to stop forthwith. I appealed against the order and was granted a public enquiry which turned out to be more of a farce than anything we had ever attempted to mount on stage. Hundreds of friends turned up in our support and only the unhappy couples who had brought the action about sat miserably in the front row.

The hearing went against us but we appealed against the verdict and this time we won; the only qualification was that the number of productions should be kept 'within reasonable bounds', though that phrase was never defined.

And that has been the situation ever since. These days we get requests to mount more rather than fewer productions because broadcasting work, as you shall discover, began to make greater and greater demands on available time.

[18]

The events covered in the last chapter spanned more than twenty years so to resume the main thread of the story it's necessary to go back to the period of my life in which 'Saturday Club' played such a prominent part.

One aspect of the programme was one referred to by the production team as the joke opening. How and when this came into being I can't recall. In those days there were mercifully no such things as jingles and station identification was made verbally, while almost all programmes had their own signature tunes. We thought that something extra was needed to grab attention and hold the audience that had been listening to the previous programme. We began to devise thirty-second sketches which always ended with some such line as 'Welcome to "Saturday Club" ' and no doubt we all thought them funnier than anyone else might have done.

Now I have always prided myself on doing impressions of people. I'm not in the Rory Bremner class, let it be admitted, but nevertheless I'm sufficiently good at some voices to raise the odd laugh at parties or to play practical jokes by telephone. In my repertoire in the late fifties was a passable attempt at the distinctive sound of John Snagge, chief announcer and voice of doom for national disasters. He had an instantly recognisable way of prefacing the gloomiest of news with the words, 'This is London.'

You are probably ahead of me by this time. The Saturday morning arrived on which, at ten o'clock, I uttered in solemn tones the hallowed words, 'This is London. It has just been announced that in millions of homes throughout the country', pause for effect, then switching to own normal voice, 'people have switched on their radios to listen to "Saturday Club".' Signature tune.

Now that may strike you as extremely innocuous today, for we live in an age in which images of the royal family and of the cabinet are regularly laughed at on television. But as a measure of the seriousness which attended my own 'joke opening' I can tell you that it made headlines and caused shock waves. My own solicitor rang me to say, 'You bloody fool. You almost gave me a heart attack. I was just getting into the bath and when I heard you I thought war had been declared.'

The following week I was summoned to the office of my boss Jim Davidson, who took me to task in no uncertain terms. He then read an unbelievably pompous letter from John Snagge saying that he found it hard to believe that someone who had once been a member of his staff could be guilty of such bad taste and appalling lack of discretion. Jim continued to berate me for a while, extracting a promise that I would never do such a thing again, then just as I was leaving his office he stopped me by saying, 'Of course you know what was really wrong with it, don't you, Brian?' 'No, Jim,' I replied. 'It was too bloody good,' he said.

So that one I got away with. The next one, I'm happy to say, I didn't. I had a call in my own office one day from Cliff Adams, who has a long and admired reputation as the founder of several vocal groups and choirs. He ran the Stargazers, whom some people will recall, and surely everyone has heard today of the Cliff Adams Singers. Well, Cliff was also gainfully employed in organising and recording advertising jingles for commercial television, and he had been approached to find a narrator's voice for a new campaign for Murraymints. They were at that time running a series of animated cartoons depicting among other things a platoon of guardsmen singing, 'Murraymints, Murraymints, the too good to hurry mints.' I gather research showed that the cartoons were immensely popular, but sales figures were disappointing. So, a change of style was envisaged with a much more direct approach and hard–sell technique. Cliff asked me if I would be interested in being the voice. Of course he knew as well as I did that this was absolutely taboo for members of BBC staff but when I reminded him of the fact he merely said, 'Well, no one need know. And I won't tell anyone if you don't.' So I agreed and was shortly to be heard extolling the virtues of the aforementioned sweets with great regularity, for this was a big campaign. I was to learn that in some quarters at least my own voice was as recognisable as that of John Snagge.

So once again the summons came to visit senior management, but this time my offence was rank and I was called to Jim Davidson's boss, the supremo of Light Entertainment, Pat Hilyard. He wasted no time saying that it had come to his notice that I had broken a golden rule and in my craven anxiety I denied the whole thing. It wasn't my voice on the commercial, I lied. Yes, there was a similarity, I realised, but it was just someone else who sounded like me. Confronted with this Pat, being the true BBC gentleman that he was, didn't know quite what to do with me. He therefore relegated the whole matter back into the hands of the much more direct and down to earth Jim Davidson who wasn't going to be put off with any of my nonsense. He told me that I might be able to pull the wool over other people's eyes, but not his. He knew damn well it was me, he said; personally he would like to be able to say good luck to me, but he couldn't. He therefore suggested that I might consider resigning from the BBC as the only honourable course.

This caused considerable heart-searching on the home front, for although I was not well paid at that time at least I had a regular job, with prospects and a pension fund. In our dilemma Pamela and I consulted an old friend from the amateur dramatic society with whom we were by this time associated; she told us to take the bold approach and go ahead. She warned me that if we didn't, we might spend the rest of our lives regretting the decision and wondering what might have been.

When my resignation was in I crossed over to the other side of the BBC fence, and although there have been the almost inevitable hiccups experienced by most freelance employees I cannot say that I have ever for a moment in the past thirty years wished that I had decided differently.

[141]

An acquaintance from the music publishing business suggested that my immediate need was an agent and introduced me to Paul Cave, who at the time handled the career of Frankie Vaughan, then by way of being a superstar who could fill the Palladium, made hit records and had just starred in a film opposite Marilyn Monroe. Paul agreed to take me on, but unfortunately he immediately decided to change the direction of his own career and left the management office in the hands of others with a good deal less flair. Nevertheless, they did negotiate my first contract with the BBC, who were keen for me to continue to introduce 'Saturday Club' and 'Easy Beat' and were, it seemed, willing to pay me about four times as much as they had when I was a member of staff.

Immediately I was on the open market I was approached to introduce programmes for Radio Luxembourg as well. The structure of that station in the early sixties was rather peculiar. All programmes were transmitted from the Grand Duchy where a few disc jockeys were in residence, but most of them were recorded in London. Some were made in Radio Luxembourg's own minute studios in Hertford Street, Mayfair, while the rest were in the hands of record companies who bought air time to do with as they pleased. They all followed the same pattern, putting together programmes of records that were only on their own labels, naturally, but beyond that they tried to cram in as many titles as possible so that everything was faded after just over a minute and as many as a dozen records might be squeezed into a fifteen minute slot. The companies working like this were EMI, Decca, Phillips and Pye and between them they used the services of Pete Murray, David Jacobs, Jimmy Savile and Alan Freeman. I was contracted to Pye to share their rota of programmes with Kent Walton and I soon found myself introducing eight of these a week in a mixture of fifteen and thirty minute slots. It sounds quite a lot but they were all scripted for me and we knocked them off in half a day at Pye's own studios at Marble Arch.

The Artists and Repertoire manager at Pye was a delightful man who was also named Alan Freeman, though he was unrelated to the famous 'Hi, Pop Pickers' broadcaster. This Alan had started as an independent producer in the record industry and had almost immediately shown flair and skill by making a successful record with Petula Clark. Unfortunately he needed co-operation from a major label to ensure distribution of his product and was, alas, squeezed out of business. So he joined Pye records, then managed by Louis Benjamin, and took Petula Clark with him. She was destined to become one of their top hit-making artists for many years and was soon followed on Alan's list by Lonnie Donegan and later by Kenny Ball's Jazzmen.

At around this time there was a television programme called 'Thank Your Lucky Stars' which was produced by ABC TV and screened on Saturday opposite the BBC's 'Juke Box Jury'. Pop stars were seen 'performing' their hits and new releases, though in fact they mimed to their records, then they in turn would introduce a newcomer. That at least was the original concept, but it was soon due to change. The programme was hosted from the beginning by Keith Fordyce who had joined Forces Radio in Hamburg just before I left.

My friend Alan Freeman devised an insert for 'Lucky Stars' to be called 'Spin-a-disc' in which three teenagers would listen to new releases and then award them points from one to five. A second host was deemed necessary to deal with this feature and Alan took me along to dinner with the show's director, Philip Jones, who agreed to take me on.

Although an ABC production, the programmes were actually recorded on Sundays in a studio belonging to Alpha Television in Aston, Birmingham which, to fulfil a stipulation made by the ITA, provided facilities for half its working week for ABC and the other half for, I think, ATV. So we all travelled in a sort of motorcade – artists, presenters, directors and designers – up the M1 early on Sunday mornings and returned late at night.

For a while the two-presenter format worked satisfactorily and then an unforeseen problem arose. Actors Equity, the trade union, called a national strike against ITV and ordered all members to stop

[143]

work immediately. Keith Fordyce was a member and complied with the order. I had not paid membership dues for nine years, from the time we went to live in Holland, and as I sincerely and firmly no longer believed myself to be a member I saw no reason to strike and became the sole presenter of 'Thank Your Lucky Stars'.

I was about to be introduced to the dirty tricks department of union politics. Equity informed me that non-payment of dues, even for nine years, merely meant that I was a lapsed member. Retirement from the union, they told me, only came with death or written application for an honourable withdrawal and, as I had not fulfilled either of these requirements, I was summoned to explain myself before the full council.

My management were all for me fighting this matter in court and took me to discuss the problem with a lawyer. He, too, fancied the challenge and thought I had a very strong case, but agreed with me that, if we went to court, in the final analysis the outcome would depend on the arbitrary decision of a judge. There was no clear-cut legal distinction between right and wrong, and there could be no guarantee of success. I decided to go it alone and agreed to face the council.

They had certainly assembled all the big guns. Margaretta Scott, whom I had seen as Portia in Stratford, still seemed to be playing the part, though she wasn't so hot on the quality of mercy this time and seemed to be all out for my pound of flesh, blood and all. Boyd QC, alias Michael Denison, also made an impassioned speech for the prosecution and André Morell, looking solemn and belligerent, asked whether I was not ashamed for having betrayed my fellow actors. No one appeared to sympathise with my firmly held belief that I was no longer a member of the union, though when I was sent out to await the verdict Richard Attenborough joined me to say that he thought I had been shamefully treated, but his plea for leniency had been ruled out of order. Many years later other distinguished members of the theatrical profession then present confessed to me that they shared Richard's views.

My sentence was that I be suspended for a year and that I pay nine years' back subscription to be re-instated. There was also a possibility that, during my year's suspension, other members could be instructed to refuse to work with me. This would have put even my radio programmes at risk and effectively made me unemployed, but fortunately that particular threat was not carried out.

The only positive aspect of the matter, from my point of view, was that I continued to introduce 'Thank Your Lucky Stars', and when the ITV strike was settled poor Keith Fordyce was not asked to return. At the end of the year, on payment of back-dated dues, I was re-instated as a member of Equity in good standing and have remained so ever since.

I stayed with 'Lucky Stars' for five years and enjoyed most of the experience enormously. Early on in that period we accidentally discovered a 'star' of our own on our Spin-a-disc panel in the person of Janice Nichols, a young lady with a broad Brummie accent who, when she liked a record particularly, would say, 'Oi'll give it foive!' It soon became a national catch-phrase as an expression of extreme approbation; to this day people still ask me who was the girl who used to say those words in such a beguiling fashion. Janice became a regular on the show as did a young man from Liverpool who has become a professional broadcaster himself for Radio Merseyside, Billy Butler.

One experience I shall never forget. An American singer who appeared one week was an all-in wrestler named Frankie Townsend; he had made a record called 'I'm the Greatest' long before Muhammed Ali made that his by-line. The record promotion man thought it would be a great idea for Frankie to perform the song in a wrestling ring, throwing me about the while, and I rashly agreed to go along with this. I was duly sent along with this man-mountain to Dynely rehearsal rooms in Marylebone where he put me through my paces for a couple of days. He first seized me in a head mare, then body-slammed me a few times, completed the routine by holding me across his shoulders for an aeroplane spin, then threw me out of the ring. During this rehearsal I was thankfully dumped every time on a mattress, but Frankie said, 'You'll notice that I

[145]

bang ya down a bit harder every time, but you'll find it hurts less after a while.' He could, as they say, have fooled me.

When the day of the recording came I did an off-screen announcement of the bout between Frankie and The Hooded Twister, then made an appearance in ludicrously long wrestling shorts and a full black hood, completely dwarfed by the real wrestler. At the beginning of the bout I feigned to bite his hand, whereupon he ripped off my hood, revealing my identity and inducing squeals of anticipated terror from young fans in the audience. The fight and the song continued according to plan and as I was duly thrown from the ring I was caught by stagehands and made the link into the next item lying on a stretcher.

Townsend's record wasn't a hit, but I was! The following week Bill Butler said, 'Hey Bri, that wrestling was dead good. Me mates in Liverpool all used to think you were big 'eaded, but they reckon yer all right now.' Praise indeed.

At the beginning of my 'Lucky Stars' years I used to drive to London, leave my car outside ABC's offices, which were in Hanover Square, and then travel in a company car to Birmingham with Alan Freeman, and usually with a guest DJ who appeared with the youngsters on the Spin-a-disc panel. At the end of a long day under studio lights a drink seemed highly desirable but as we were situated in one of the less salubrious areas of Birmingham the local hostelries offered little temptation and there was barely time to reach anything further afield before closing time. Then the problem was solved in the most extraordinary manner.

One Sunday Kent Walton was the guest DJ; at that stage of his career he was much better known for his television wrestling commentaries. As we sat in the back of the car speeding away from Birmingham he told me that once, when leaving a wrestling venue with a couple of the contestants near to closing time, they just made it to a pub with minutes to spare. They simultaneously ordered two rounds each and were set to smash them down in quick time when they were invited to step into a back room and to stay as long as they liked. Not long after he had finished telling me the story we arrived at a huge pub called the Old Malt Shovel at Stonebridge, halfway between Birmingham and Coventry. We just had time for a drink and then, to my astonishment, we were invited to step behind the bar and through a door into a restaurant area with bottles of scotch and gin on several of the tables. The landlord, who introduced himself as Billy Walker, treated us right royally to both liquid and solid refreshment and we stayed well into the small hours.

Thereafter for many months we made this watering hole a regular point of call, always with the same treatment, and as the word went around more and more members of the 'Lucky Stars' cast would come with us, and more and more members of the public turned up as well to gawp at them. It wasn't long before this necessitated a move into a much larger function room and it didn't take Billy long either to talk his guests into singing for their supper. The most bizarre assembly I recall in that whole period was when Kenny Ball's band brought in their instruments and played a set and the Springfields sang, to the delight of more than two hundred drinkers. I wondered if this wasn't making the whole thing a bit too public, but Billy assured me all was well and pointed out the Chief Constable among the happy revellers.

Undoubtedly the most nerve jangling programme of all was one on which The Beatles appeared. Beatlemania was already approaching its height and there was no way we were going to get away with this one quietly. The whole day had to be planned with military precision and the studios in Aston prepared almost as if for a siege. On advice from the police the plate glass front of the building was completely barricaded with planks and sandbags and pavement barriers were erected to help control the anticipated crowds. We were all ordered to rendezvous with the Boys' car some ten miles out of Birmingham and from there we drove in convoy under motor-cycle escort. In the event everything passed off smoothly and without incident but from that point on it was very strange to be involved in the pop music side of entertainment. Crowds grew larger and were for the most part younger. They came along to scream, to work themselves into a frenzy. There was no possibility of listening to the music, however loudly it was played.

After five years of 'Lucky Stars' I became immensely tired of the nonsense and sick of the hysteria. It all seemed to me to have little or nothing to do with entertainment and when I let this antipathetic feeling show the management deemed it best that I be replaced. They were right.

Long before that happened, though, there had been much to enjoy and remember. Like the young fan who, one Sunday, presented me with a tiny black kitten named Pepe, asking me to give it a home. It was a pathetic little creature, but thrived and grew into an eccentric cat destined to live with us for some years. Slow in reaction it was unable to catch birds, for which we were rather thankful, but did manage once with a prodigious leap to land on the back of a large, startled pigeon. Less startled, however, than Pepe who fell back in astonishment at his unprecedented success; the relieved pigeon escaped.

Unaccustomed as I was at first to the workaday world of television I was dumbfounded by the extent to which the division of labour was jealously watched by the various unions involved and the speed with which a demarcation dispute could flare up. I used to sit, for example, on a high stool for most of the links between items, playing straight to camera at fairly close range so that position had to be accurate to a nicety. On one occasion the director asked me to move two inches camera right and without thinking about it I got down from the stool with the intention of moving it. Before I could do so, a couple of chaps rushed at me from the side of the studio and asked me what I thought I was doing; that, they informed me, was 'work' for props and if I attempted to touch the stool they would come out on strike. I thought they were joking, but they weren't.

The original director, Philip Jones, was quite keen I remember on having a visual gag at the end of the programme, over which he could roll closing credits. On one occasion the last artist on the show was the late Billy Fury, singing his hit song 'Halfway to Paradise'. The set for this was a large, sweeping staircase, centre stage, running down from a balcony. Bill started the song on the balcony, and gradually came down the stairs to the floor, where I came into shot and thanked him, then went up the stairs closing the programme, with a final wave from the balcony. At this point I was to lean back on the rail, which had been sawn through, and disappear over the back. This meant a drop of a few feet, after which I should land on a strategically placed mattress. It worked well at rehearsal and, fortunately, I checked it out before the recording to discover that some charming anonymous worker had slipped a stage weight under the mattress. It could have been extremely nasty.

There was another instance in which I was made a scapegoat, but this is one that I recall with pleasure. During the week prior to a show the director rang me at home to say that we had been given an unexpected opportunity of trailing the programme live on air. There was a two minute gap in the schedules that would occur in our own break between rehearsal and recording. Would I, therefore, write a script and send it, in triplicate, to him?

Now this was unusual, but not at all illogical, and shortly after his call there was another from the lady in artists' booking who confirmed the time and arrangements and discussed the fee with me. So, on arrival, everyone knew that there was an extra item that day which only involved me and camera crews. At the appointed time a call was given to clear the studio of all but those of us directly concerned. I duly sat in front of camera, watched the clock tick up to the minute and, on a hand cue from the floor manager, went into my routine, believing myself to be addressing the nation, live. Then out of the corner of my eye I saw another figure coming into shot, just behind my shoulder, and to my horror a female voice began to ask for my autograph. Feeling like death I kept a presenter's dreadful plastic professional smile on my lips and tried to ask the intruder to wait until I had finished. She wittered on inanely and I kept going, with mounting horror, to the end of the allotted span. The longest two minutes of my life. Then the director emerged from his cubicle, grinning hugely, and told me that I had just been on 'Candid Camera'. For a few seconds the air was blue as I vented my wrath on him, but of course the joke continued as the cameras were still rolling and this was the funniest bit of all.

When I calmed down I was invited to see the recording and then asked if I gave my permission for it to be used. I said I should be delighted for it to go into a programme as it was definitely the funniest thing I'd ever done.

There was one more element which made this far and away the busiest part of my life up until now. My manager suggested that pantomime would be a useful career development and fixed me to play Idle Jack in *Dick Whittington* at the New Theatre, Bromley, which was run by a director named David Poulson. This theatre, incidentally, was burned down a few years later and made way for the building of the Churchill. On my first day with the rest of the cast there was a faint air of antagonism on their part. Implicit rather than vocal, but recognisable for all that. They confessed later that they resented a famous disc jockey coming along to try to be an actor, but happily this was soon dispelled when they realised that I had had both training and experience.

It was ironic that I should be playing Idle Jack at a time when anyone less idle is hard to imagine. To start with there was the panto, then I had to go up to London on two or three occasions during the week to pre-record sessions for 'Saturday Club'. Transmission for that meant a six a.m. start, followed by two pantomime performances, then off again first thing on Sunday morning for the 'Lucky Stars' telerecording in Birmingham. We somehow also managed to squeeze in the eight programmes a week for Radio Luxembourg and one other for BBC Transcription Service which was and still is to this day called 'Top of the Pops', though it's totally unconnected with the television programme of the same name.

Most of the things I'd ever heard or read about performing in pantomime turned out to be more or less true. Arthur Askey was spot on when he said the very word conjured up for him the smell of oranges and wee-wee, and he wasn't a million miles from the mark when he said that the Principal Boy's big solo number was usually a signal for a mass and noisy exit to the lavatories. I discovered for myself that after the first couple of weeks of what had seemed like really hard work it all got a lot easier and that when that point had been reached most actors would start to improvise and ad lib in a fairly outrageous sort of way. I don't think this was ever taken to the point where the show was spoiled for the audience and it certainly added to the amusement of those taking part.

The handsome actor playing the Dame, Sarah the cook, stood with me at the back of the stalls on the first day of rehearsal eyeing the members of the chorus and weighing up their attractions. Having gazed at the Fairy Queen for a moment or two he bet me ten shillings that he would have his way with her that very night. On arrival the next morning he calmly announced that I owed him ten bob. And having recounted that story, perhaps I'd better let him remain anonymous in mine.

It was also during this panto period that I met an actor named Arthur White who has remained a good friend ever since. He wasn't in the show, but had a wonderful store of knowledge about really funny comedy business and devised for us a superb arms drill routine that always brought storms of laughter. He and I were later to act together in a new play and he also produced Pamela and myself in *Rattle of a Simple Man*. It was through Arthur, too, that we first met and acted with his younger brother, later to achieve massive and deserved success as David Jason.

My own activities at this peak period were to go on for a few years without too much change, but when change did come it was cataclysmic.

[19]

Our new-found affluence, relatively speaking, had by this time started to change our lives in many respects. First of all we had to do something about Christopher's schooling, as he didn't exactly seem to be flourishing at the local junior school to which we had sent him. We were warned that he would be unlikely to pass an eleven-plus examination to the grammar school which then existed, for although he was bright enough he wasn't all that good at application. It was suggested that he might fare better at a private school.

We found a prep school near Sevenoaks called the New Beacon, some ten miles from where we lived, with a mixture of day boys and boarders. Christopher was very impressed with what he saw, especially bunk beds in some of the dormitories, and insisted that he wanted to board. With the benefit of hindsight I should not make the same decision again for I think the whole concept of boarding school is wrong, though the Beacon was as good as many and better than most. We also became close personal friends of the family who had founded and ran the school at the time and Christopher claims that generally speaking he was happy there.

His greatest achievement was learning to drive without any instruction, merely by having watched us. We discovered this when attending an open day. We stood around on a lawn, knocking back the sherry, when a message was brought to Mr John, the Head Master, known to us all – and the boys – as Johnty. He came to us and said, 'Don't panic, but Christopher is driving your convertible round the lower playing field.' The boy obviously had to be rebuked for his misdemeanour, and as he had never taken any more kindly to that than his father before him, he decided to run away from school. Very slowly though, as Johnty duly reported. He had no intention of not being overtaken and returned to the fold.

While Chris was at this school we became owners of the first in a succession of boats which have been both blessing and burden in our lives ever since. We took him to an Earls Court Boat Show merely for an outing and of course went aboard a variety of craft. One that took our fancy was a twenty-three foot single engine cabin cruiser and no doubt we lingered over it more than over other exhibits. Pamela, who has always been our chancellor of the exchequer and cautious by nature, made no commitment and we eventually left the show. Walking back to the car park Chris was unusually silent for a while, then burst into uncontrollable tears. 'Whoever heard of anybody', he blubbered, 'going to a boat show and not buying a boat?'

We went back the next day and bought it!

The new pride and joy was named *Chrisje*, which is a sort of Dutch diminutive and is what friends called our son when he was a baby in Holland. We took delivery at a marina called Penton Hook on the Thames, near Windsor, and kept the boat there for a couple of years. My plan was to try to learn navigation from books and practice without simultaneously having to learn to sail and then in due course to change to sail. It is indeed what eventually happened but it took far longer than originally anticipated.

After a while we planned to have the boat transported by land through France and launched at the small harbour of Cassis, close to Marseilles, for a couple of weeks' holiday in that part of the Mediterranean. We loaded *Chrisje* with everything we might require in the way of clothes and food for the proposed holiday and set out with small son and a young friend of ours by train, via Paris, to Cassis. On arrival we discovered with horror that the boat was still in England, where it remained on a broken down trailer in Dover till our return. There was no way we were going to do without our holiday altogether, so we booked into a small hotel and, despite having only the clothes we stood up in, had a marvellous time. Chris met up with a youngster of his own age whose father had a sailing boat lying at anchor just outside the harbour, so we even got a little boating in as well.

This failure to achieve our objective persuaded me that the next move should be to a larger twin diesel engined boat that we might ourselves take across the Channel and through the canals of France. So a trade-in was organised and this time we became the owners of a second-hand cruiser named *Espada* and moored in Chichester Yacht Basin. It had three cabins, and a centre cockpit with a canvas hood.

Espada carried us happily about the Solent area for a while, and we learned the very different demands made on boat handling and navigation by tidal waters and we spent many happy weekends pottering around the Isle of Wight and further afield to Swanage Bay, where we had friends with a hotel.

Then came the long-planned ambitious trip, to and through France, with the intention of leaving the boat in the Med. for a lengthy period. The crew was to be Pamela and myself with Christopher and an American friend of his from school, which was Mill Hill by this time; and young Mieke from Holland also spent her usual summer with us.

For the Channel crossing we took along another man to share the fairly long spells at the helm with me and set off in reasonable conditions from Chichester for Cherbourg. My navigation was accurate on this occasion and Cherbourg harbour mole came up right on the nose; we settled in for the night and my helper during the crossing left next morning for the return by ferry to England. The rest of us set out, sailing west to round the headland and then steam south to St Malo where we planned to enter the canals through Brittany.

When we were somewhere in line with, but not in sight of, Jersey we lost one of our engines. It transpired that it was merely out of fuel, as there were tanks on both sides with a connecting pipe, but the valve had been left closed. I decided to change plan and put into Jersey to sort out the problem; fortunately a passing fishing boat offered to guide us into the little port of Gorey. This dries out at low tide, but at that stage I didn't know *Espada* could sit on the bottom without rolling over and so decided to stay outside for the night. We took her in on the next high tide, after a rough and sleepless night, and soon resolved our problems, enabling us to set out once again for St Malo. I should have waited another night and tried to gather local knowledge about the very strong currents in that part of the world but instead found out the hard way. Long before we closed the French coast, darkness fell and I found it far harder than I had imagined to identify the flashes of the lighthouses. In fact, we were lost. I sounded into a bay, with shore lights visible, and put down the anchor. Then, while everyone else went to their bunks for some sort of sleep, I kept anchor watch for another restless night. With daylight we were more easily able to identify our position and set out again for St Malo, this time successfully; we finally passed through the huge hydro-electric dam near Dinard to get into the inland waterways.

All went well for a few days, with plenty of locks to keep us busy and pleasant little towns to visit. Then disaster struck again. A large commercial peniche approached us in a fairly narrow section of canal and it was only when he was on top of us that I could see his bow wave sucking down the water level at the banks. We must have dropped a metre in height, my starboard propeller hit the bottom and pulled its shaft clear from its engine mounting. We had no option but to limp along with one engine until we neared Nantes and there found a French boat builder, M. Cahils, who kindly offered to help. He hoisted me on to his slipway, took out the bent shaft and damaged prop, and we spent the next five days living aboard at a very strange angle while repairs were effected.

Ostensibly fixed up again, we set off once more and at Nantes passed through another lock to take us into the river Loire. The plan was to journey down into the Bay of Biscay, then follow the coast south to the Gironde and at Bordeaux to re-enter the waterways, travelling by the Canal Latéral du Midi all the way to Marseilles and the Mediterranean. It's a trip I should still like to do one day!

The first part of the journey on the Loire was pleasant and easy, but after an hour or two conditions deteriorated and we started to take a lot of water over the top. I clung desperately to the wheel while Chris bravely stayed on deck with me swabbing as much as possible down the drain holes while the others remained below. Eventually a river authority launch came close to hail us and directed me into a quayside at the small fishing town of Paimboeuf where smock-clad fishermen rushed out to take lines and make us secure. It had been an anxious time, neatly summed up by a French yachtsman I met later. 'Ah, the Loire, monsieur,' he said, 'when the wind is against the tide, the waves are square.'

After a rough and restless night, the day dawned calm and peaceful. We set off once again and this time, with an unpleasant bang, the supposedly mended prop shot out of its housing again. For a second time we limped on with a single engine and made the port of Le Croisic, where *Espada* was hauled out and patched up. By this time our plans had to be ruthlessly altered, as we were taking on two other friends who were joining us for a fortnight's holiday, so on advice from local experts we made for the island appropriately called Belle Île and spent a couple of weeks pottering about there.

The American school chum of Chris's had thus far turned out to be a bit of a pain in the neck or, to make analogy with another part of the anatomy, what his own countrymen would term a smartass. He had shown great reluctance to wash, was nowhere to be found when locks approached on canals and, disobeying orders when we were lying at anchor in France, had gone over the side to swim in a fierce current and got swept a long way before managing to cling on to another boat until I could rescue him. His derisory term for me on most occasions from first coming aboard was 'brave captain'.

During our stay at Belle Île we made occasional trips between the main harbour of Le Palais, where we took on fuel and water, and the smaller harbour at Sauzon, which was mainly occupied by private boats. In Le Palais we once lay alongside the yacht belonging to Princess Grace of Monaco. It was slightly smaller than the *Queen Mary* and carried on deck a seaplane as big as we were.

On one of these passages between harbours, some distance off-shore, a crew member drew my attention to a lobster pot marker flag which appeared to be following us at some speed. We had obviously gone over a connecting line and wound it round one of our propellers. I stopped engines and, donning mask and snorkel, grabbed my sheath knife and went over the side. By making numerous dives beneath the boat I was eventually able to hack clear the fouled prop and climbed back up the stern ladder.

There to greet me on the stern deck, with ill-concealed astonishment mingled with new-found respect, was my young American guest.

'Gee,' he breathed, 'you really are brave captain!'

By the time we got back to the mainland I had run out of holiday. We got the boat back to dear old M. Cahils in Nantes, then I flew home leaving Pamela and the boys in charge. After hair-raising adventures that would fill a book on their own they got back to Jersey, then to Cherbourg from where the boys were plucked back to school and where Pamela and a friend managed to pick up a sailor (!) from a Royal Navy training yacht who volunteered to navigate the journey back home to Chichester. He insisted on the girls handling the boat themselves; he did the chart work and spent the rest of the time sitting on the rear deck playing jazz on a trumpet.

Soon after this *Espada* was taken round the coast to the river Medway and moored at a small marina in the non-tidal part of the stream. I am ashamed to admit that she was sadly neglected there and began to look rather sorry for herself. Amazingly, a couple of men stepped on board when I was paying a rare visit and asked if they could buy her. They made an offer I couldn't refuse and we closed the deal. As a footnote I often see *Espada*, which now has a solidly constructed wheelhouse in place of the canopy, moored in Maidstone. She is obviously a resilient old lady, if rather frail by now, and I can only wonder at the adventures we had aboard her.

There followed a boat-free period for a couple of years until the bug reasserted its presence. I took a dinghy sailing course in Poole

Harbour and then we both went on a dinghy sailing holiday in Minorca, where Pamela discovered the delights of trapezing on a racing boat. On our return we found a little twenty-one foot sailing cruiser which we bought and thoroughly enjoyed for about five years. It was followed by a succession of ever larger boats, all named 'Round Midnight', culminating in the present, and almost certainly the last, vessel – a lovely thirty-six foot Westerly Corsair capable of going anywhere, which is sadly no longer true of her owner. She did play a significant role in our lives in the spring of 1990, as you shall see at the end of this story.

[20]

We have to return to the 'Saturday Club' saga at this point for one of the most extraordinary events of my broadcasting career. It was also connected with the BBC Transcription Unit and their programme 'Top of the Pops', which I have already mentioned in passing, so perhaps this is the time to explain just what that is.

'Transcription' was originally conceived as a source of income for the Corporation; programmes would be sold to other broadcasting organisations worldwide. It differs fundamentally from the World Service which transmits from England by short-wave; its output is recorded and then transferred to discs which are flown out to be broadcast locally by the customers. For many years it was not possible for Transcription to utilise gramophone records, and so they were obliged to use studio recordings made for domestic broadcasts in Britain.

'Saturday Club', of course, filled the bill beautifully from their point of view since about four fifths of its content came from our own sessions. Pop music had not, up to that point, featured in Transcription output, which was of a much more serious and classical nature. Someone, however, had the foresight to realise pop was about to become a tremendous force with worldwide appeal just at the very moment when British pop was leading the field.

An American distribution agency, which already handled plays and concerts, saw the huge potential of programmes in which the Beatles, the Rolling Stones and others could be heard performing live rather than on commercial disc. Between them and the BBC Transcription Unit, 'Top of the Pops' was conceived with myself as compère. Funnily enough, we never did get it off the ground in the

States but it soon became the Unit's biggest seller and it still is. After more than twenty-five years I remain the compère and although we now make the programme from commercial discs it is currently to be heard in about fifty countries.

Back in the early sixties, however, the Beatles were just about to make their second tour of America and as the BBC knew of my association with Brian Epstein on the theatrical side they asked me if I could arrange to join part of the tour myself. Brian readily agreed and fixed me up with a seat on the private charter plane carrying the team from venue to venue, and with accommodation in the same hotels. It was guaranteed that I should have daily access to the boys to record interviews so that this material could be despatched daily to the agency in New York for nationwide distribution. There were also two or three American DJs on the plane, but none of these was granted anything like the same facilities.

I was to stay with the tour for a week and perhaps it's worth mentioning the rather bizarre fact that for the few days before departure I was playing Shylock in *The Merchant of Venice* and was due to make one more appearance in the role on the very day that I got back. I had not until then had any experience of jet-lag.

The Beatles were already in the States when I left London, but Brian had marshalled my arrival wonderfully. As I entered the airport after landing a tannoy announcement called for me and I was hustled through immigration and customs like a VIP, to find a limousine waiting to whisk me into the city.

After settling in I made my way to Shey Stadium where the boys were to appear before a vast audience. This one I wanted to experience from the front, so I stood with my recorder on the baseball terraces and watched the Beatles land in the arena by helicopter. The noise was incredible and after the first chord of each song had been identified the rest was completely drowned in screams and yells. Back at the hotel after the concert John Lennon admitted that they hadn't been able to hear themselves either and were just swept along on a huge wave of excitement.

Graham Nash (The Hollies)

Paul Jones

Pete Townshend (The Who)   Matt Monro

Petula Clark

Georgie Fame

Dusty Springfield

Marianne Faithfull

Interview with '70s star David Essex

Left: Self as Baron Stonybroke in panto. *Right*: as 'Himself' in the 'Scottish Play'

Henry and Eleanor in *The Lion in Winter*

Left: Helping Lord Bernard Miles reopen the Mermaid Theatre. *Right*: With José Ferrer at the Chichester Festival Theatre

Left: Arthur Mitchell, Director of the Dance Theater of Harlem, in New York for 'Round Midnight'. *Right*: On the Radio 2 Float in the Grand Parade at the Edinburgh Festival, 1986

Two scenes from *Same Time Next Year*, the Neil Simon play in which a couple are seen on one-night stands at five-yearly intervals

Left: Steve Race and John Dankworth present me with the Wavendon Allmusic Award as Radio Personality of 1988. *Right*: Back to the stage in 1990. As Justice Shallow in *The Merry Wives of Windsor* at Chichester

As 'Pa' in Snoo Wilson's play *Lynchville* at the White Bear, Kennington. *Above* with John Cassidy and *below* with Laurel Lefkow and David Whatley

It wasn't possible to record much at the stadium, but I did get one line that has since been used in many a compilation. Standing beside me was a short, fat, owlish Jewish boy with a wonderful accent. I asked him which was his favourite Beatle, and without so much as a pause for deliberation he said, 'John Lennon. He has a kind of eloquence without being eloquent.'

The worst part of the whole experience for the Beatles themselves was that they were total prisoners. Their every whim was catered for, but they were not free to step outside their hotels and it would indeed have been dangerous for them to do so. At concerts there were armed guards on the approach to their dressing rooms, they had to stay there once inside and food was brought to them; transport between hotel and venue was frequently unceremonious to say the least. I asked Brian if we could arrange for me to be with them for the whole procedure on at least one occasion and this was fixed for me in Chicago where the show was to be given at the Komisky Ball Park.

Under very explicit instructions, with synchronised watches, John, Paul, George, Ringo and I stood in readiness in our separate rooms. Outside the front of the hotel was a huge crowd of fans hoping to see and possibly to touch their idols. On a given signal, a decoy car came to the front of the building while we were hustled down back stairs and literally thrown into the back of a shooting brake; we were told to lie flat until clear of the hotel. In this highly uncomfortable position I managed to record the thoughts of the four boys until we arrived at the venue. The police manoeuvred the car through gates in a high wire fence which had countless bodies pressed against it and many more squeezing in behind. I think it was George Harrison who made the remark that they were in danger of coming through like chip potatoes.

Once out of the car, the stars had to make a dash for the tunnel to the diamond while cops with sticks stood on guard. As I brought up the rear one of these representatives of the law grabbed me by the arm, raised his stick to whack me over the head, and said: 'Where ya goin', mac?'

[161]

Fortunately, Paul turned round in time to gasp, 'S'all right, 'e's with us,' and pulled me in behind him.

The most alarming display of Beatlemania that I saw during the entire tour was at the Maple Leaf Stadium in Toronto. Girls were not only screaming but fainting clean away. Those who remained passed the inert bodies over their heads and the unconscious were laid out in serried ranks in the corridors. It was all a manifestation of immature sexual passion, but there was nevertheless something rather frightening about those strained, tear-stained faces.

The best night of all was in Atlanta, Georgia where, despite temperatures in excess of a hundred degrees at midnight, we were treated to a sumptuous southern meal after the show with fried chicken, black-eyed peas and all the trimmings. The worst night was on our arrival at the airfield for Houston, Texas. It was extremely late, we had all been drinking on the plane and for the first and last time in my life I had succumbed to an invitation from the American DJs to pop a few mysterious pills. Security here was at its most lax and a horde of fans surrounded the plane, climbed on to the wings and flicked cigarette ends into the night sky. It's a miracle we were not all blown to kingdom come. Ringo broke the tension on board by shouting in his droll fashion: 'Beatles and children first.' At last some sort of semblance of order was restored and we were driven to our hotel.

After checking in, I was wandering along a corridor searching for my room when a door opened and several female arms reached out, grabbed me and hauled me inside. No, it wasn't a kidnap, or even an 'old mannap'. Three fans had succeeded in capturing a member of the Beatles party and wanted to talk about their idols. When they discovered that I actually knew the boys and had with me recorded interviews with them they insisted on a world première, right there in their room, before I was released.

The end of the week arrived all too soon, and while the entourage moved on to Los Angeles I flew back to London. I was met at the airport and whisked to Broadcasting House where 'Saturday Club' was being introduced by Simon Dee; there I gave an impromptu up-date on the American tour, then dashed over to Kensington House in Shepherd's Bush to record a report for the Transcription Unit. After that I was driven home, wearing shades to disguise my bloodshot eyes, slept for a few hours, then got up to play Shylock once more. That performance passed without much awareness on my part yet an actress friend offered her verdict that it was the best thing I had ever done. I still hope she wasn't right.

At about this time I had the first of a succession of unpleasant surprises to rock my self-satisfied complacency. When I left the shelter of BBC staff to freelance I was asked to continue as compère of 'Easy Beat', but it was pointed out that I couldn't go on producing the show. Was there anyone, I was asked, whom I could recommend to take over? My immediate suggestion was the studio manager who had worked with me on that show and on 'Saturday Club' for a few years. He got the job, and almost immediately decided to make his mark by getting rid of me and replacing me with Keith Fordyce. A long time later, at a rather bibulous party, he apologised profusely and confessed somewhat tearfully that he had always regretted his action and hoped that we might someday work together again. We never did.

As we came towards the late sixties I was also removed, as I have explained, from 'Thank Your Lucky Stars'. That, however, was a loss cushioned to some extent by my manager booking me for the first of two years to present Sunday concerts at the North Pier, Blackpool. The mixed bill had acts that I no longer remember, but we closed the first half with Bert Weedon and topped the bill with the late Matt Monro who had had a huge hit with his record of 'Portrait of My Love'.

The North Pier Theatre was at the seaward end of the pier and a very long walk from the shore. There was a lugubrious stagedoor keeper who would invariably greet us with tidings of doom, whatever the weather. 'Yer'll not 'ave many in tonight,' he'd say. 'It's raining. They'll not walk all this way in't wet.' Or alternatively: 'Too 'ot. They'll not come along 'ere in this.' We soon realised there was no way we could win in his book, but thank goodness he was way off the mark and we enjoyed a tremendously successful season.

Matt Monro was a delightful man with whom I had the pleasure of working on numerous occasions and we always got on well together. He was of small stature and always made jokes against himself about this in stage presentation. During this season Pamela came one week to see the show and brought young Christopher with her. In the car, after the show, Chris suddenly asked, 'Daddy, who was that dwarf who came on dragging a hosepipe?' When I reported this to Matt the following week he loved it and immediately incorporated it in his act.

Some years ago I was honoured by the Songwriters' Guild who awarded me their gold badge of merit for outstanding services to music. On the same occasion, a badge was awarded posthumously to Matt; his widow Mickey came to receive it. She made a marvellous and gracious speech and threw us all into hysterics when she said in conclusion, 'And if Matt were here to receive this himself, I know he would have said... about bloody time.' He would, too.

I went back to Blackpool with a far less illustrious bill and didn't enjoy the experience half as much. Some compensation for this, though, came from the fact that my old friend Clinton Ford was playing the full season at the Central Pier and with his wife Maggie had taken a house. They generously put me up there on Sunday nights and he and I enjoyed many a convivial night after the show. One outrageous night we didn't go to bed at all and in the early dawn made our way to the pleasure beach on the south shore where we climbed all over the big wheel and untied all the boats in the tunnel of love. Then on to the beach where we watched a man on a bicycle about a mile off shore. He was, it transpired, riding through the shallow water of low tide to collect bait for fishing, but it was still a very strange sight.

And so the decade meandered on towards its close and with it the end of BBC Home, Light and Third as I had known them, and the advent of Radios One, Two, Three and Four.

Robin Scott, smug and snug on the management floor, decided he was happy to take 'Saturday Club' into the Radio One fold for a while but not to take me with it. From the beginning of the sixties when I had had two hit shows on radio, a television programme, panto and summer season, here I was at the other end with only my Radio Luxembourg programmes left. For a while I experienced black despair, but not, fortunately, for very long.

[21]

A former Light Programme producer, Brian Willey, who had been a close colleague for several years was the first to come to the rescue. He said he was shocked by the cavalier way in which I had been removed and asked if I should like to work on his daily afternoon programme 'Roundabout'. At that stage this general interest and music magazine had a different compère each week but Brian soon changed the routine to use me on alternate weeks, then for a month at a time and eventually made me the permanent host.

The basic format for the show was to have contributions by various regulars covering film, travel, astronomy and so on, while the resident compère introduced the music and conducted occasional brief interviews. These were sometimes extended by design and sometimes by an exceptionally extrovert guest taking over. As when Warren Mitchell appeared, live, in the dreadful persona of Alf Garnett and kept up the character throughout. He occasionally let me off the hook by wandering to the studio door and shouting such lines as 'I'll be back in a mo' Bri', I'm just goin' dahn the karzy.' Then he would leave me to try to restore some semblance of order before he returned to recreate havoc.

Warren, of course, is a superb actor whom I had known at the Royal Academy and far too much of a professional to let this get out of hand. He simply gave a very funny performance which injected a welcome fresh element into that day's programme.

I was also intrigued to meet the Israeli actor Topol who not long before had been the toast of the town as Tevye in *Fiddler on the Roof*. He had also negotiated a contract that gave him an interest in the show even after he left it as a performer; his role was taken over by the late Alfie Bass. During the interview I asked Topol if he was going to Her Majesty's to see the show. 'I don't need to go,' he told me in a manner that struck me as rather self-satisfied, 'I know how Alfie plays the part.'

A great advantage of being on 'Roundabout' for some years was that it allowed me to become actively involved in theatre again, provided I could work within easy reach of Central London. One rather ambitious project that Pamela and I undertook was to mount a production of *Hamlet* which we then toured to various schools, including Mill Hill where our son Christopher was a pupil at the time. Attendance at the performance was not compulsory but on this occasion the hall was full. A very nervous and ashen-faced Christopher came backstage before the show to apprise us of this fact and Pamela quite naturally said, 'Good.'

'It had better be,' was the fearful response.

After the very successful performance, however, he came back again to admit all had gone well. 'They all thought Dad was good,' he reported, 'but they asked me who was the crumpet playing Ophelia. That wasn't crumpet, I said, that was my Mum.'

I think Pamela felt rather flattered.

At about this period I also renewed acquaintance with the great master of stage make-up Richard Blore, who was a world-wide demonstrator for Leichner and who at the time ran a studio or sort of make-up clinic just off Leicester Square. It occurred to me that it might make an unusual item for the programme if I went along to this studio and asked Richard to create something especially difficult and to record his own commentary on what he was doing to me. A little bizarre for radio, perhaps, but it worked quite well. Happily it also allowed me to find out that Richard was in charge of the intimate Bromley Little Theatre where productions ran for ten days in each fortnight.

Over the next few months we took in productions of *Who's Afraid of Virginia Woolf?*, *Uncle Vanya* and *The Lion in Winter* and I directed *As You Like It* in a set as near as I could get to a simulation of Shakespeare's Globe. Pamela also directed an

[167]

adaptation of Hans Andersen's *Snow Queen* with and for youngsters.

Richard used to collect me in his car as soon as I came off the air at Broadcasting House, then drive like a bat out of hell to get me to the theatre just about in time to get ready for the performance.

We also returned to Bromley New Theatre, where I had played Idle Jack in pantomime, to appear in the wonderfully funny *Rattle of a Simple Man* which had been such a hit in the West End starring Sheila Hancock and Edward Woodward.

Altogether this was an immensely enjoyable period of life but of course it had to come to an end eventually. The decision was made to axe 'Roundabout', which caused a minor public outcry but as in all such changes management knew from experience that they only had to keep their heads down till the flak stopped flying.

For a while it became more than a little difficult to maintain a foothold in radio as a broadcaster but I managed to eke out a living as a contract producer overseeing music recording sessions for a variety of programmes. In fact I was asked to build the music for the Jimmy Young show when he first moved, rather reluctantly, from Radio One to Radio Two, but thankfully that didn't last very long. How on earth anyone puts up with such a boring chore for any length of time and considers themselves a producer I can't imagine. However, I was never totally off the air and for a while hosted the long established 'Late Night Extra' for one night a week; at another period I introduced an hour-long magazine called 'After Seven', but that never really took off and didn't last long either.

Then came an opportunity to get involved with another daily programme that was to absorb an enormous amount of time, but also gave me a great deal of pleasure. It was called 'Album Time' and each day presented reviews of newly released LPs. My first producer on this was that lovely lady Lilian Duff who had for many years been a distinguished broadcaster herself, introducing an esoteric record programme called 'Continental Cabaret'.

'Album Time' was another programme that alternated compères for a while, but here again I eventually took it over completely.

My final producer on the show was a man nearing retirement who had for much of his career been a music studio manager, Jimmy Dufour. He had managed to retain both his own jovial personality and a fresh approach to anything he undertook. We were constantly on the lookout for new angles and broadened the scope of the show by going out to record interviews covering the manufacture and the retail side of the record industry, as well as technical developments such as, for example, the Dolby system of noise reduction.

During this aspect of our work we met a man who had bought a small company that specialised in low-price products, most of which he acquired from other people's back catalogues. However, he asked us if we would like to produce some new children's material and we jumped at the chance. Pamela did most of the script adaptations, we rounded up a small company of actor friends, I rented a studio at the BBC Transcription Unit and we turned out one set of albums of dramatised Andersen stories and another of the Grimm Brothers.

Then real disaster struck. We were to have a dinner party at home and before any of the guests arrived I was in the bathroom when, quite without warning, I experienced something which I can only describe as an explosion inside my head, followed by the most excruciating pain imaginable. I lay on the bed and was quite unable to attend the dinner. In fact I had to send down a request for quiet. Eventually it became apparent that this was no ordinary headache and a doctor was sent for who immediately gave orders for me to be rushed to hospital. She suspected, and subsequent tests proved, that I had had a brain haemorrhage.

I have virtually no recollection of the next few days when, it transpired, it was a fifty-fifty chance whether I pulled through or not. When I was fit to be moved I was transferred to the Brook Hospital where they specialised in illness stemming from the nervous system and I was put in a ward with other patients suffering from brain and spinal defects. At first it was thought there would have to be an operation which involved the removal of the

[169]

top of the skull, but fortunately further tests showed that this was unnecessary. I had to lie prone for a couple of weeks while nature took its own course, and this was followed by a period of convalescence. Basically there are two kinds of brain haemorrhage, one occurring inside the organ which renders operation more or less essential; the other, which I had suffered, is termed subarachnoid and takes place in the membranous covering of the brain. Though it is serious, there is less likelihood of side effects such as facial paralysis, which of course would have spelled the end of my career as broadcaster or actor.

The staff at the Brook were absolutely wonderful and in my own case I was especially well looked after by a West Indian nurse named Ella who was kindness personified. She had a large family of her own and still found time, perhaps from economic necessity, to perform this great public service. I have never forgotten her.

During my convalescence Pamela played the role of chauffeur and we toured a little of the West Country, particularly visiting the Dart which I remembered with deep affection from my childhood. Recovery was rapid, but as I was unable to take much exercise I'm afraid I put on a disgraceful amount of weight at least some of which has been removed during the ensuing years.

On the work front two completely unexpected events kept us afloat just when help was needed. A department head at BBC World Service had telephoned Pamela when he read of my hospitalisation saying that he would do whatever he could to help when I recovered. He was as good as his word and employed me to write and produce a daily programme linking the date with historical events and relevant music. It was introduced by Margaret Howard, the voice of 'Pick of the Week', and was a most pleasant programme. This also led to programmes of my own on World Service which were to continue for several years.

At the same time I was contacted by a man who had been in advertising but had bought out the record company for which I made the children's records I mentioned earlier. He said he wanted to release them and to pay me a royalty, could we meet and discuss?

Needless to say I agreed at once and our initial meeting brought about many other projects. He told me that he had put out an Australian recording of songs of the war years which had done so well that he wanted a follow-up, preferably with a Guards band and chorus. I asked him to give me twenty-four hours and was able to offer him a package that filled his needs. I had worked in radio with Captain Peter Parkes, then the director of the Grenadier Guards Band, and he offered to provide me with a band culled from the brigade, plus recording facilities in the Guards chapel. Clinton Ford was added as soloist and I hired the mobile recording van from Transcription Unit. The result was 'Great Hits of the War Years, Volume Two' and, advertised on television, it did very well.

I then went on to record an album of cover versions of great instrumental hits and another of famous movie themes. Both of these made the album charts and then I was asked to collate an album of guitar hits to be recorded by Bert Weedon; although I didn't actually produce the studio sessions for that one I was credited as executive producer and 'Twenty-two Golden Guitar Greats' went to number one.

Whilst busy making these records I was also invited by the BBC to be the holiday relief for Terry Wogan on his morning show; that was an offer I couldn't refuse. It was a daunting task for, whatever one thinks of his television programme, he was brilliant on radio. However, it seemed to go well without too much audience complaint and indeed I was asked back again on later occasions.

At this time Christopher was managing a garage in West London and had rented a fairly large basement flat near Regent's Park. I was able to stay with him for a couple of weeks, rising at six to drive to Broadcasting House for the Wogan programme, then going straight on to recording studios for the rest of the day and often much of the night as well. It was all very stimulating and there wasn't time to feel tired.

My World Service activities at this time had developed into a programme called 'Matthew on Music' master-minded by a producer named Humphrey Walwyn who tended to be a shade erratic but was brimming with ideas. He eventually left the BBC to join a commercial record company, since when I have lost touch with him. However, during our period of working together we did many interesting things; one that stays in my memory was a visit to the country home of the brilliant guitarist Jeff Beck who sat beside me on his settee and gave the most amazing master class of rock guitar playing I have ever heard.

This series proved enormously popular all over the world and eventually Humphrey sold the idea of him and me travelling to the Far East with the two-fold purpose of studying the extent to which western popular music was having an effect on the indigenous music and also of investigating the extent of piracy of recorded cassettes going on, especially in Hong Kong and Tokyo.

Humphrey set off to Calcutta, Djakarta and Bangkok, then met up with Pamela and myself in Hong Kong from where we flew on to Tokyo. I think we were able to fulfil our brief to satisfaction and it was certainly a wonderful opportunity to see these exotic locations.

In Hong Kong we met up with a young accountant friend who had acted with us in England some years previously. He was working for an Australian tax avoidance company and his boss owned a beautiful junk converted as a private motor yacht. Westerners were obliged by law to employ a boat boy in these waters, and we were taken out for a fascinating trip, anchoring for a memorable picnic in a secluded bay of Hong Kong overlooking Kowloon on the mainland.

We were also invited by an employee of Hong Kong Radio to attend a private dinner being given by a very wealthy friend of his. When we arrived at the venue, we found several parties of Chinese seated at round tables where they were all playing mah-jongg, a noisy gambling game accompanied by much clicking of tiles and jabbering, and quite illegal in Hong Kong. Of food there was not a sign and we were bade to sit at a table on the side where there were full bottles of gin, scotch and brandy and told to help ourselves until such time as the gambling came to an end. Then, on a signal, the mah-jongg ceased and the equipment disappeared as though by magic. An army of waiters came in and at that point we noticed a sort of tower in another corner. It was in fact a table, but with about a dozen table tops piled upon it, each ready complete with place settings. These were lifted down and distributed to the gaming tables and there followed the most delicious twelve-course dinner the like of which I have never experienced before or since.

Another highlight of this part of the trip was a visit to the film studios of Run Run Shaw, where literally hundreds of films were turned out yearly for distribution not only throughout the East but also among the Chinese communities in the States. The supremo was a tiny, immaculately dressed man with the inevitable inscrutable face, almost lost behind a huge desk in his vast office. He gave us a fairly comprehensive account of the enormous output of his studios and we were able to visit some of the lots where shooting was in progress; at the end of the day we witnessed the amazing spectacle of the workers' exodus by bicycle to the overcrowded part of the Territory in which they lived.

This very overcrowding means, naturally, that every available site is built up and among other things this renders arriving at and leaving Hong Kong airport a nerve-racking experience. As we took off with Japanese Airlines for Tokyo we could literally see straight into the offices and apartments in the surrounding highrise buildings.

The work schedule in Tokyo was much heavier and precluded our seeing as much of the country as we should have liked. On arrival at the airport we began to wonder whether we should in fact even get into the country at all. Immigration took longer than anything experienced anywhere else in the world, and for the first time we realised that when a Jumbo touches down with a full load it is almost like the arrival of the entire population of a sizeable village.

The next problem was one of which we had had advanced warning. Japanese streets are named but buildings have no numbers. The mind boggles as to how post gets delivered, and life is not easy either for non-Japanese-speaking westerners confronted by a non-English-speaking cab driver. How we ever did find our hotel I can't remember.

The next shock about Tokyo was the high level of smog in the city. This derives partly from the climate but largely from the horrendously dense traffic; even the policemen are equipped with smog masks. We soon discovered, too, that though a morning may dawn bright and sunny, by about eleven o'clock the majestic Mount Fujiyama had completely disappeared from view.

Another surprise was the minute size of the hotel bedrooms, with beds nowhere near long enough for us. In the one where we stayed it was also impossible to open the windows, despite excessive central heating. Perhaps things are better if one can afford to go considerably more up market than was possible on our allowance.

Most of our working days in Japan were spent in studios, either interviewing or being interviewed. I found, for instance, that my transcription programme 'Top of the Pops' was very popular on one of the commercial stations and they were delighted to put me on air. On one free morning, however, we were able to visit an extraordinary robot-operated FM station in a skyscraper. Four white-coated assistants spent their days compiling record pro-grammes on tapes; these were then fed into a wholly automatic process, where mechanical arms picked them up, laced them up and started them playing. A computer organised the insertion of commercials and controlled the availability of microphones for newscasts.

Being firmly of the opinon that radio works best as a means of personal communication I was rather appalled by all this and asked one of the few human beings on the station what happened in the event of a break-down. 'Is no problem,' he assured me. Then indicating another glass-fronted bank of equipment he added, 'There is complete duplicate, Number One breaks down, this take over immediately.' I hadn't the heart to ask what happened if they both went off the air.

On the day of our departure we were taken to dinner by a couple of businessmen who unwittingly endorsed something we had already learned; the Japanese are not the greatest drinkers in the world, but they do try to render their guests legless. These two poured saki down us like it was going out of fashion, which for my money it's very welcome to do, but managed to get themselves into a perilous state in the process. One of them seemed intent on persuading us to carry an important message back to our western brothers. 'Preese,' he begged, 'you are terring Engrish people we rove rittle dogs. We do not eat rem, we rove rem.'

The return journey was as memorable as anything in the trip; we flew over the North Pole and put down for refuelling in Alaska. Landing at Anchorage in a blizzard and mighty low temperature we were obliged to leave the plane and go into a reception area where the first thing on view was a huge polar bear, standing erect and holding out its forepaws in a fairly menacing manner. In a glass case, of course. I wonder if it's still there.

There is one other story that rightfully begins in this chapter, though it will continue through the whole of the next, and that is the beginning for me of a love affair with Edinburgh and the Edinburgh Festival that was to continue uninterrupted for thirteen years.

A producer named Ian Fenner with whom I had previously worked on 'Late Night Extra' rang me to ask whether I would be interested in going to Edinburgh for ten days to broadcast two programmes from and about the Fringe and to record a third for later transmission. This seemed too good an opportunity to miss, but I had no idea at that stage just how important it was going to be for me.

The Fringe Club that year was in a building in the Royal Mile, just below the castle, and it was from there that we were destined to broadcast, in far from ideal surroundings. The place was packed to capacity nightly and as all the accommodation was on the first floor and above, the thought of evacuating in the event of fire was too alarming for words. In more recent years much tighter restrictions have been enforced and not before time.

Being part of the Edinburgh Festival Fringe is a form of intoxication and it's extremely habit-forming. I don't think I should ever have kicked it had the decision not in a way been made for me, but that's another story. Suffice it to say that David Hatch, now the Managing Director, radio, first went to Edinburgh with Cambridge Footlights and he always manages to get there, year after year, if only for a few days.

In my first year there I was part of a team of some seven or eight from the Light Entertainment department; we stayed in an ageing hotel in Princes Street not far from the Scott Monument. We met up each morning for breakfast in the dining room where we had the luck, or perhaps misfortune, to draw the oldest, most decrepit and accident-prone waiter in the establishment. He was rapidly christened McManuel. Other waiters would clear a table from previous occupants like lightning, loading everything on to a huge tray and carrying it at one go to the kitchen. As they approached the swing door they would half turn, kick the door smartly with one heel, then spin round and rush through. On our first day, perhaps with some misguided idea of impressing us, McManuel tried to emulate this trick of the trade. He loaded the tray almost beyond the point of being able to lift it, staggered to the pass door and delivered his kick, but turned round far too slowly to have any chance of getting through. The door swung back to meet him full on and sent him and the tray flying. He didn't have another go at that.

One of the great things about the Edinburgh Fringe is that it gives an unrivalled opportunity for members of the public to be in on the birth and burgeoning of new talent and it was my good fortune on this first visit to see early performances by Rowan Atkinson. He had gone to the Festival with the Oxford Revue company and a show that was ill-prepared. There was a major dispute within the group and most of its members decided not to go on, but Rowan, with the help of a musician, mounted a one-man show that was a tremendous success and paved the way for more of the same the following year.

In those early days of his career Rowan suffered from a difficulty that I think he has probably overcome by now. Although he could speak fluently in performance on stage, in an interview he

[176]

developed a bad stammer which he was quite unable to control. I have only come across this problem once or twice, usually in people of marked creative genius, another example being the theatre and television director, Bill Bryden. It's as though their thought processes move at lightning speed, far outstripping the power of speech.

Some few years before all this I had experienced at close quarters the very different problem of the decline of a once good and active brain. In his late seventies my father began to suffer from arteriosclerosis, or hardening of the arteries, which leads among other things to loss of memory. In his case he seemed able to recall his own childhood with clarity; at the same time he was unable to remember something that had been said but minutes before. By the time he reached his eighties this became a great burden for my mother and when it was physically impossible for her to care for him he had to be taken into hospital. He was sent home, however, when the end was considered to be near and eventually died in his sleep in his greatly loved little house.

My son was eighteen when his grandfather died, but volunteered to drive me to Coventry to attend the funeral. He was a tower of strength and saw me through a devastating period. My mother insisted on my going to the undertaker's parlour to see the body which I scarcely had the courage to do, but Chris took me there and held on to me while I went through this rather grisly and meaningless ritual.

I wanted the funeral service to reflect the two things that Joe had always loved best next to his family, brass music and Shakespeare. The conductor and many members of the Coventry band gave up time to play at the service and I read Prospero's farewell speech from *The Tempest*, but could barely manage to complete it through the tears. And finally, in accordance with my father's wishes, his ashes had to be scattered on the sea at Dawlish. Chris was with me for that as well and he will probably never realise just how much his support meant to me during one of life's inevitable but most distressing experiences.

[177]

[22]

The longest and most personally rewarding chapter in my broadcasting career began in January 1978 with the birth of a programme called 'Round Midnight' originally designed to coincide with the introduction of twenty-four hour round the clock broadcasting by Radio Two. Ray Moore was contracted to look after the early morning show which, although he took long breaks from time to time, he continued to introduce until shortly before his tragic and untimely death. I took the other end of the day and stayed with the programme until it was eventually terminated some twelve years later.

'Round Midnight' evolved into a very different programme from the one first envisaged; the changes were to some extent brought about by a succession of editors widely varying in ability and imagination. But to put it in perspective it is necessary to introduce the remarkable character who was responsible for setting up and nurturing it through many a difficult period. His name is Steve Allen.

A cockney born and bred, Steve has now retired from the BBC but we worked together for many years. I first knew him as a studio manager, one of our team on 'Saturday Club'; he then went on to become a producer responsible for a number of jazz programmes. One outstanding series was called 'Hear Me Talkin' to Ya' for which he recorded long interviews with jazz stars, then edited out his own contribution so that the jazz musicians alone did indeed 'talk to ya'. Steve achieved a notable success in this way with Louis Armstrong quite late in his life, but he often told me with a chuckle that the funniest bits were those he deemed best left on the cutting room floor. Louis was legendarily preoccupied with his bowels and when Steve asked him how it was that he was able to continue playing although by then of advanced years he replied, succinctly, 'Keep shittin', man.'

Steve himself was a semi-professional trumpet player and for a while augmented his income by fronting a small dance band. In this capacity he once put in a band for me at a pantomime I directed in the village hall. One front cloth act was presented by two young men whose enthusiasm far outstripped their material. They appeared as Bill and Ben the Flowerpot Men, once famous on children's television, and, standing behind cut-out flowerpots, did a rather pathetic cross-talk routine during which the laughs were few and far between. After several minutes one of them ill-advisedly introduced his next gag with the line, 'Here's a joke.' Steve's endurance had by this time long been stretched to its limit and he responded from the band with a very audible, 'Abaht bleedin' time.' For that indiscretion he was known forever after to Pamela and myself as 'Bleedin' Steve'.

As a producer he made the European Broadcasting Union his area of special interest, which gave him the opportunity for many expense-paid trips abroad. Thanks to his generosity with person-ally exported bottles of the amber spirit to which he always referred as 'The Scottish Wine' Steve's fame and popularity soon spread throughout Scandinavia. To be fair to him, despite a somewhat bizarre vocabulary and delivery ('I fink I can resolve vis dichotomy gent'men' was an example), he had a flair for diplomacy and learned to play the management game to perfection. As a result he was promoted to the role of Executive Producer and so he remained until there was a radical change in the structure of his department.

There are few who would refuse an invitation to lunch from Steve and I am certainly not one of their number. He was quite a gourmet, liberal with the wine, and always an amusing companion. He it was who made the initial approach to me with the idea of introducing a live three hour programme from eleven p.m. to two a.m. for five nights a week. The contract was for a year with an

[179]

option for a second and there was an attractive guaranteed minimum salary. I had no hesitation in accepting straight away and never regretted the decision for a moment.

At first the suggestion was made that there should be two presenters, myself and a woman broadcaster, and that we should make a practice of answering personal problems on air. That's a style I deplore, for observation has proved to me that late night programmes of that kind attract many cranks, and those presumptuous enough to offer their advice and suggestions almost invariably seem to be least qualified to do so. I resisted that idea and won the day before we went on air.

The next slight hiccup arose for technical reasons. When the starting date arrived in January 1978 it was still not possible to launch all night transmissions and we had to go ahead with a one hour programme for the first three months which I presented from a continuity suite, playing the records myself which is now of course widespread practice in broadcasting everywhere. I ceased to do this, however, when the three hour programmes arrived because we wanted to be able to use live musicians in the studio on occasions and also to involve three and sometimes more guests simultaneously for open discussions.

It seemed to me at the outset that a resident script writer for special features would be extremely useful and the way in which I found one seemed almost like the hand of fate. I had previously met an Australian named Frank Salter who had been employed for a while on 'Roundabout'. Originally a ballet dancer with the Australian Ballet he first came to England with Laurence Olivier after an Old Vic tour and worked as a company manager during the early years of the National before the move to its South Bank home.

Frank was a man of great culture as well as being a wit with a fine writing style and a memorable turn of phrase. I have occasionally been praised for skill at lifting the written word from the printed page and I knew that, for me anyway, Frank could write words that were eminently liftable. Anyway, shortly before we were due to start broadcasting I met him in a West End street purely by chance;

when I asked after his welfare I was horrified to discover that he was unemployed, hungry, and had literally ninepence in his pocket. I supplied him with ready cash to keep the wolf from the door and sped off to find my first editor, John Molloy, to persuade him to hire Frank. He readily agreed and so our writer joined the team and a great asset he was for several years. Many a time we would be short of a guest or an idea and at a minute's notice Frank would pound away on his typewriter, producing a feature that looked as though he had spent a week on it. Eventually he yearned to return to Australia to write a book about Borovansky, who had founded the Australian Ballet and had been Frank's boss and mentor. He wrote the book to critical acclaim if not for great financial reward; but alas, he never returned to England, as he had developed emphysema. I kept his flat on for a while but eventually the landlords, the Church Commissioners, wanted it for another tenant and obliged me to let it go.

One very strange thing happened during the early days of 'Round Midnight' and has never been satisfactorily explained. I am still unhappy about it for it smacks of government intervention and unwarranted censorship.

Once, when deputising for Jimmy Young, I met and interviewed Jeffrey Archer about his first novel, *Not a Penny More*. During our conversation it became obvious to me that Jeffrey was not only steeped in the lore of the House of Commons but also loved it dearly, with all its tradition and ritual. Remembering this I suggested we ask him to make weekly contributions to 'Round Midnight' in the form of a plain man's guide to the mystique of the House. He was very happy to do this and I thought he complied with the brief beautifully, translating the jargon into lay terms and making it all very understandable. He has never made any bones about where his political allegiance lies, but neither did he make these broadcasts an opportunity for party propaganda.

After several weeks of this feature John Molloy received a directive from on high ordering him to discontinue using Archer. We were told quite bluntly that this was not debatable, but an instruction that brooked no argument and came initially from the government Chief Whip's office. It would have been interesting to hear Jeffrey's own explanation of that little bit of parliamentary procedure, but I never had the opportunity to talk to him again till many years later he acquired the Playhouse Theatre, and that didn't seem to be the right occasion.

One of the things discussed when we were setting up the content of the programme was the Edinburgh Festival. I pointed out to Steve that the programmes I had introduced from there the previous year had been in what was now our time slot. He saw the point at once and talked the idea through management so that we were scheduled to visit the Festival for two weeks to broadcast every night from Broadcasting House in Queen Street in the Scottish capital. Three hours was far too long a programme for the purpose and as we were feeling our way at that stage there was much padding, with irrelevant records and tapes between the Festival items. But it was a start, and led eventually to programmes that I think were unique.

In the second year of the programme the production team was joined by Keith Harrison, a young man who had been a broadcaster himself with a daily stint on the local station, Radio Cleveland. I think his hope in moving south to headquarters was to get a programme of his own on network radio, but if so he was disappointed. After a while he left the BBC altogether and took a post as an announcer on Channel Four.

During his spell with me Keith was instrumental in setting up some of the lighter elements, and organised for me a memorable interview with Mohammed Ali. The great boxer was by this time past his prime but still had not fallen to the sad level that was ultimately to be his lot. He arrived in the studio with two bodyguards who were giants even by comparison with mightly Ali. They both quite blatantly carried revolvers in shoulder holsters under their otherwise immaculate suits and stood quietly if ominously slightly behind me during the recording.

Some sixth sense had told me that this could be a difficult

situation so I had taken steps to give myself a chance. There was at this time on the BBC canteen staff a young and very beautiful black girl who always chatted to me when I was on a meal break. I asked if she would like to meet Mohammed and she bubbled over with enthusiasm, so I installed her in the control cubicle behind Ali so that he couldn't at first see her.

After he had been introduced to me he sat at our table, put his head on his folded arms and feigned sleep. He was obviously wide awake, but reacted to my first question with a slight grunt. Before things got out of hand I asked if he would like to meet a really beautiful girl and up came his head. 'Where?' he wanted to know. 'Behind you,' I told him.

He took the bait exactly as I had hoped, and after a deeply growled, 'Wow', demanded that she be brought into the studio. She sat beside him for a while, clearly thrilled to be there and he didn't look displeased either. He now started to take more interest in the proceedings and, perhaps to show off to the girl, came up with some interesting answers. When it was all over and she had gone back to work Mohammed looked me straight in the eye and said, 'You a ver' wise man.'

Another unusual guest Keith lined up for me was a hypnotist named Martin St James. He did an entertainment show in theatres and clubs, but he had also set up anti-smoking clinics around the country. His main reason in agreeing to appear on my show was to give air to grievances over what he considered unfair treatment by a Sunday newspaper; as a result he had lost a lot of work. In brief, a girl who had attended one of his theatre shows had died shortly after returning home. Despite the fact that she had not been one of the subjects taken on stage and put under hypnosis and notwithstanding a heart condition, confirmed by her doctor, this Sunday paper published a banner headline over a photograph of Martin's eyes, 'Are these the eyes that kill?'

Not long after he went to Australia to play a series of engagements on stage and television only to discover that the newspaper story had preceded him and all his bookings were cancelled.

[183]

When he appeared on 'Round Midnight' I was an extremely heavy smoker, getting through up to sixty Camels a day. I had been persuaded once before on 'Roundabout' by Steve Race to give up the disgusting habit, but went back to it after a couple of years. If asked, I always used to maintain that I truly enjoyed smoking and had no wish to give it up again. During the course of the St James interview there were, as usual, several full packs on the table in front of me. At one point he said to me, 'Don't worry about me, light up if you want to.' I didn't, and when the recording was over he said, 'You must be dying for a cigarette now. Go ahead.' To my astonishment I had no desire to smoke at all and have had none from that day to this.

This story was too good to pass up so I made a bonus of it and called Martin back to explain what he had done to me. 'You've taken away one of life's little pleasures,' I accused him. He replied that he had done nothing at all and claimed that I had subconsciously wanted to give up and had used him as a sort of catalyst. 'You stumbled on the secret', he said, 'of self-hypnosis.'

Needless to say we were inundated by calls and letters from listeners demanding to know who this man was and where they could find him. We directed many people to him, but unfortunately I never heard of anyone else who had a similar experience. So, had I discovered self-hypnosis or not? All I can say is, not only have I never smoked since, for over ten years now, but I find the smell of tobacco quite repulsive.

The next dramatic development for the programme occurred after I had taken a holiday in California. Pamela and I went first to San Francisco, then for a couple of days to ghastly Las Vegas and after that to Los Angeles. A British film director I had met, John Hough, was making a movie called *The Black Hole* for Walt Disney studios and had invited me along for a visit to the set. While there I also renewed acquaintance with the historical novelist Rosemary Anne Sissons who was negotiating a script deal. Then an American musician who specialised in South American music and folk instruments took us on a guided tour of parts of Hollywood seldom seen by the average tourist. For lunch she had booked a table in the restaurant of the music centre overlooking the theatre; it was known as the Mark Taper Forum. Her motive was for me to witness at first hand a remarkable live lunchtime radio programme in which the host sat at a table with three or four guests from the world of the arts and conducted a conversation with them, on air, while they had lunch.

This struck me as such a good idea that I could scarcely wait to get back to try it on the then managing director radio, Aubrey Singer. My suggestion was to mount it overlooking the river Thames from a table in the restaurant of the National Theatre, but Aubrey had other ideas. 'I like it, Harry' he said. For some reason he never did find out my name and always called me Harry, 'Set one up right away and let's see how it goes.'

'Thanks, Aubrey,' I said in some surprise, 'when can I do it?'

'In your own time slot,' he said.

Now this struck me at the time as the height of absurdity. How could we mount a live audience show in the middle of the night?

We were soon to find out.

The first venue John Molloy chose was the Crucible Theatre, Sheffield. On the night he decided to make the broadcast, the main auditorium was housing a folk music festival so there would be several artists on hand, including the incomparable Jake Thackray, and we could also do an in depth feature on the theatre itself.

To our total astonishment not only was there a large audience in readiness for us but many of them stayed till the end of the second hour and even into a little of the third. We were off to a flying start on this the first of the outside broadcasts of 'Round Midnight' of which I eventually lost count.

The next one proved something of a disappointment because no one turned up at all. As an audience, that is. Had it not been for the fact that Pamela brought over my mother and a friend from Coventry we should have felt very lonely. The show was set up in the circle foyer of the Royal Shakespeare Theatre in Stratford-on-

[185]

Avon, but although we had put up plenty of posters and banners, the audience leaving the show in the theatre passed us by without displaying much curiosity.

It was on that occasion I decided I never wanted to do another audience show at which records would be played. We didn't charge for admission, but if I had anything to do with it from that point on we would always put on a real show, with live musicians performing between the interviews. It was more difficult, but vastly more rewarding, and it worked. By the time we put on my last show, again in the main house in Stratford, in early 1990, the stalls were full and remained that way until one o'clock in the morning. On this occasion our music was mainly from the wonderful production of *Showboat* being presented jointly by the RSC and Opera North. Furthermore, in an unprecedented gesture that I shall forever appreciate, Terry Hands came up specially from London to congratulate us, on air, for all that we had tried to do for theatre generally over the years.

There have been two other regular venues for 'Round Midnight' over the years: the Belfast Festival and the Chichester Festival.

The event in Belfast is spread over a whole month but compared with Edinburgh the attractions are fairly thin on the ground. Set against that, however, it was instigated more than twenty-five years ago by students at Queen's University and they have continued to play a part in keeping the festival going. Leading international artists are prepared to attend and there have been regular visits by touring groups from both the RSC and the National Theatre.

My own shows in Belfast have usually been for two nights only and with one exception when we played in the Little Theatre, which I thought was ideal, those shows have been in Broadcasting House and in part of the University adapted for the Festival as a folk club. I shall never forget our first visit as long as I live. Ralph McTell was one of the artists booked to appear for us, and when he launched into his famous song 'The Streets of London', the whole packed audience joined in with him. For once the hackneyed old phrase 'there wasn't a dry eye in the house' was totally justified.

When it was all over no one wanted to leave and young people came up, held our hands, and thanked us for coming to Ulster. They just couldn't understand that we felt they were doing us a favour.

I must make mention of a Belfast pub called The Crown since this unique building, greatly admired by Sir John Betjeman, demanded at least one visit on all of our trips to Northern Ireland. A long bar down the whole of one side is faced by booths, each with its own door and capable of seating eight or ten. There is a bell system like those found in the kitchens of old country houses; one's call is visually displayed over the bar and summons a waiter in straw hat and apron. The decor is of painted tiles, the lighting from simulated gas mantles, the food cheap and good and the Guinness superb.

When we first discovered the delights of this watering hole the programme editor was a large, bearded, blustering but kind-hearted man named John Bussell. He and I had deep respect and affection for each other but were also prone to argue loudly and violently. A younger colleague once described us as resembling two old bulls locked in mortal combat. Anyway, after a full morning's work and with many hours to go before the programme John and I were lunching with all the other members of the team secure in the knowledge that we could afford the time to cross the road to our hotel for a nap, a shower and dinner long before we had to go on air. After numerous libations had been sampled and everyone was laughing immoderately, a waiter appeared and asked, 'Is anny of yewz here from Raddio Tew?' Bussell admitted that we all were and went off to take a phone call, returning considerably sobered with the news that Controller Northern Ireland wished to see us all immediately.

A rather subdued team shortly presented itself at Controller's office where we found an immensely affable executive determined to lavish on us hospitality in the form of large measures of Irish whiskey. I am sure he had registered our condition on arrival and it was certainly far worse when we took our leave, still, by the grace of God, with enough time to recover.

John Bussell was involved in something that took place long

before the advent of 'Round Midnight'. He had been asked to undertake the production of a brass programme called 'Listen to the Band' and, knowing my personal experience in that area through my father, he suggested me as a compère. The idea was turned down by management and John was told he had to use Charlie Chester.

'But he doesn't know anything about brass bands,' John argued.

'Yes, he does,' was the mind boggling reply, 'he used to play bugle in the Boys' Brigade.'

The day was saved to some extent and John's sanity with it when he was at least able to extract the agreement that I should write the script for Charlie to read, and so I did for a couple of years.

The lovely coda to this anecdote is that when I was booked for the job I was staggered by the size of the fee offered. Some time later, when negotiating a contract for a script of similar nature for a single programme the suggested remuneration was far less. When I quoted the precedent of the Chester programmes the booker said that had all been a rather embarrassing mistake they would like to forget. When I pressed for an explanation it transpired that when they had first seen Charlie's name on the advice note they had assumed it must be a comedy programme and had therefore been paying me the top comedy script-writer's rate. For two years.

But to get back to broadcasts from Belfast. John Bussell was again the man in charge one year when we had included among the bands in our show a jazz quartet fronted by the outstanding Irish guitarist Louis Stewart. He continued to, shall we say, refresh himself throughout the performance and finally, dangling at a precarious angle in his chair but playing beautifully the while, he whispered to one of my colleagues, 'For God's sake get me off after this, I'm knackered.' Then when the broadcast was over and the rest of us felt free to celebrate Louis returned to the hotel in which we were all staying. At least he was poured into a cab and the driver instructed where to deposit him.

Some considerable time later when we all returned to the hotel and summoned an elevator, as the doors opened there to our astonishment was Louis Stewart propped against the side muttering, 'Will somebody for goodness sake press number six?'

The last impression I wish to give is that the Belfast Festival at Queen's is an occasion of unbridled revelry and irresponsibility. It is a wonderful assembly of talented artists gathered to celebrate much that is good and beautiful in a city that suffers all too frequent examples of the darker side of life.

A totally different festival is the one mounted annually at the theatre in Chichester in Sussex. This unique building came into being through the inspiration of local man Leslie Evershed Martin, and for over a quarter of a century now has presented wonderful plays performed and directed by some of the greatest talents in the land. The first artistic director, Sir Laurence Olivier, was succeeded by Sir John Clements and he in turn by Keith Michell.

I first visited Chichester as a member of the audience to see Olivier and Michael Redgrave give stunning performances in *Uncle Vanya* with a cast that also included Dame Sybil Thorndike and Sir Lewis Casson. That was the beginning of a love affair that goes on to this day and led eventually to the thrill and privilege of performing on that stage.

When 'Round Midnight' had set a pattern of paying annual visits to both Edinburgh and Belfast we were asked to consider broadcasting from other centres and Chichester at once came to mind as offering possibilities of a different kind. The artistic director by this time was Patrick Garland, who was to remain in office for five years. During the last part of this time he was joined by the West End producer John Gale, who then carried on alone for another five years. They both appreciated the value of promotion on a nationally networked radio programme and welcomed us with open arms. For nine years we presented 'Round Midnight' in the foyer of the main house, then in 1989 gave our last show from the stage of the newly opened studio theatre, the Minerva.

Nearly all of those programmes were master minded by Stella Hanson, daughter of the famous star of operetta John Hanson, and she it was, of all the editors on the programme, who made far and away the greatest single contribution to the development of 'Round Midnight'.

Stella was with us, not as editor but as a member of the production team, for our first visit to Chichester. That year they were presenting a musical called *Underneath the Arches* which was based on the story of the great comedy double act Flanagan and Allen. Indeed, Chesney Allen was still alive and appeared in the show himself, with Christopher Timothy playing the part of Bud Flanagan. Also in the cast were several veteran comedians who were survivors of music hall and represented the Crazy Gang, the team with which Bud and Ches were almost permanent residents for many years of the Victoria Palace in London.

The shape of our programme was to consist of songs from this show, items from a traditional jazz band we had imported, and interviews with artists and directors from three productions in the season. Unfortunately the editor had seriously miscalculated the amount of material needed to fill our two hours and we were on to our last planned piece of music with more than twenty minutes to go, live on air and with a sizeable audience there in the foyer. For the first time Stella Hanson demonstrated an initiative we were thereafter to depend on for many years. She whispered to me, 'If I put Roy Hudd back on with you, can you keep going while I get something organised?' Then she disappeared into the crowd.

Roy emerged as the music came to a close and we went into a totally unpremeditated ad lib routine which seemed to go on forever but probably lasted only a few minutes – we got some laughs, anyway. Then a scribbled message from Stella told me to introduce one of the older comedians from the cast, Don Smoothie, who would do an audience participation number called 'Underneath the Bed'.

Don launched into this outrageous old music hall song and to our surprised delight the audience joined in enthusiastically. Patrick Garland wandered over to my chair and said, 'I don't believe it. Look at them. And listen.' The blue-rinse ladies who are regular stalwart supporters of Chichester Theatre were beaming, clapping and lustily joining in with Don on the choruses.

The season at Chichester starts at the beginning of May and runs through until October. After the first production has been running for a fortnight the second is introduced and they run in repertoire for a few weeks, then when the third opens the first drops out. So, by placing our broadcast sometime late in June we always managed to have available artists from the two shows in performance and another well into rehearsal. If there was a musical on the rota, then the orchestra and singers from that provided the musical nucleus for our first hour and in this way we were able to give our listeners a flavour of, for example, *The Mitford Girls*, *O Kay* and *Annie Get Your Gun*.

In 1989 the musical was to be a revival, starring Dorothy Tutin, of Sondheim's *A Little Night Music*. It hadn't opened by the time we arrived so we were unable to illustrate that show with the artists who were to appear, but Dorothy kindly came in to give an interview and Elaine Delmar sang 'Send in the Clowns'. That was the occasion on which we broadcast from the stage of the Minerva, which had just been opened, and I must say the experience filled me with an ambition to go back there one day with a play. It's a delightfully intimate auditorium and I was happy to see, during the 1990 season, that more and more people were beginning to appreciate its attractions. I hope the time is not far away when it plays every night to capacity.

[23]

During the first two years that I attended the Edinburgh Festival the artistic director was an extremely wealthy but phlegmatic Dutchman named Peter Diamond. He undoubtedly had a wide international acquaintance in the highest echelons of classical music if fewer in theatre and none, it would seem, in ballet. It has also been suggested that he was able on occasions to secure the services of some artists by subsidising the fees they were paid from his own personal funds. I only met him once and found him about the most reluctant subject I ever tried to interview in a fairly long career.

Diamond's successor was an entirely different character: the ebulliently extrovert and charismatic John Drummond, who is now the Controller of BBC Radio Three. With his wide knowledge of the arts and his burning enthusiasm to share with others the pleasure they gave him he was in my view the ideal man for the job, the best director the Edinburgh Festival ever had or could have. He worked prodigious hours, travelled the world looking for attractions, personally attended as many performances and functions as was physically possible and had both the magnetism and the eloquence to deal with the notoriously dour and tight-fisted city fathers. He would, I know, have liked to continue in office but at the end of five years he had exhausted himself. He asked for a sabbatical to recuperate, which was unimaginatively refused, and one can only feel that Edinburgh's loss was the BBC's gain.

By the time John was first active at the festival 'Round Midnight' had been mercifully cut back to two hours nightly, which made it a much more wieldy proposition. Had this not happened I think I should not have lasted the course as long as I did. However, from the word go John took an active interest in the programme and made many impressive appearances on it himself. He didn't like the idea of recording interviews and much preferred to come in live no matter how late the hour, bringing with him unlimited and bubbling enthusiasm for performances he had just seen. He also persuaded artists who had proved difficult to contact through normal channels to give me interviews. The brilliant actor Paul Schofield was one of these – by reputation a most reluctant interviewee, in the event entirely charming and extremely informative.

At first Drummond agreed to join me in the studio during my first night's programme and my last. He enjoyed the experience so much that he was easily persuaded to come in every night with a feature I called 'Director's Diary'; he even continued this practice when we made the next major change, presenting the programme for one week in a studio and, for another, live before a huge and noisy audience in the Caledonian Hotel.

This development was engineered by the previously mentioned executive producer Steve Allen who, I have already indicated, was something of a wheeler-dealer. He saw nothing wrong and a great deal that was right in bringing together parties to their mutual benefit, even if that was not in line with standard BBC practice. He had dealt with the management of a particular hotel group, arranging outside broadcasts from Gleneagles, and now saw an opportunity for broadening the relationship.* At the rear of the Caledonian, sometimes described as the Pink Palace, in Princes Street, there is a large banqueting hall called the Castle Room, ornately decorated on walls and ceiling with paintings of all Scotland's wild birds and overlooked by Edinburgh's dominating castle.

Steve worked his magic and did a deal whereby we would rent the room for a week and instal a temporary stage at one end, on

*The Caledonian Hotel was part of the same group.

which we would present an all live show for two hours every night from eleven o'clock. We booked an outside broadcast van and team from Radio Scotland in Glasgow and took with us two studio managers from London, one as balancer and the other as a floor manager in the hall. Almost from the beginning these shows were an enormous success and, because there was no charge for admission, were soon attracting crowds we had no hope of accommodating. Our reputation grew so that we started to suffer from overcrowding on stage as well, with artists and shows queuing up to be booked.

I was always a little surprised that the Caledonian, which is a five-star hotel and very expensive, tolerated the noise level generated by 'Round Midnight' and its audiences but I can only assume that nightly mention on national radio was deemed worth all the trouble.

At the outset the hotel erected a temporary bar at the back of the hall which no doubt boosted their income enormously but didn't do much for the broadcasts. A number of local worthies began to attend who were clearly only there for the beer and they didn't make my job any easier. One little 'Jimmy' started to push his way forward during one of my introductions and shouted at the top of his voice, 'Hey you! You f....n' talk too much.' At which point he was lifted off his feet by muscular commissionaires, one either side, about turned and carried unceremoniously out. The following year we had the bar moved out into the foyer.

Another annual disturbance, which became something of a standing joke to our audiences, came from a firework concert outside in the castle gardens. This event was sponsored by Glenlivet and always ended with a performance of Handel's Firework Music accompanied by the most spectacular and noisy display imaginable. This usually attracted a crowd estimated at a quarter of a million which effectively brought the centre of Edinburgh to a halt; the concert would go on until well after eleven o'clock. The first time it took us completely by surprise and we had scheduled a very quiet act – folk singer accompanied by a harpist –

at what turned out to be the zenith of the racket outside. In subsequent years we had learned to put on either an electric rock band or a brassy jazz combination at the strategic moment. You could still hear the bangs, but they were less of a shock.

Since it had always been our proud boast that we were the most eclectic programme on radio we also made the mistake, in the early days, of trying to introduce conversations with international opera stars and concert stars between the acts – but this soon lost the attention of the audience in the hall and wasn't fair to anybody. John Drummond was one of the very few people I ever saw overcome this problem, for he had the true demagogue's gift and was able to stir the populace with a well chosen turn of phrase. What a Mark Antony he might have made.

For two consecutive festivals, in addition to the BBC work, I had the opportunity of appearing on the Fringe myself in lunchtime revues. These came about through my admiration for the enormously talented Scots actor, Russell Hunter, whom many people still remember best for his brilliant television portrayal of the whingeing little cockney character 'Lonely' in Edward Woodward's series 'Callan'.

Russell, in partnership with the writer Gordon Smith, formed a company called Cacciatore Fabro (Italian for Hunter Smith) with the purpose of producing original one-man plays at the festival. The first of these, revived year after year, was called *Jock*. In it Russell played an old soldier employed as the curator of a military museum; he would deliver his personal views on aspects of Scottish history interspersed with pithy comments on all manner of subjects. I'll never forget the sardonic grin with which he said, having pulled the ring from a can of beer, 'The first note of the great Scottish Symphony.'

The next play I saw was called *Xanadu* in which the tortuous thought processes of a man incarcerated in a mental hospital were explored; this was followed with a black comedy, *What a Way to Go*, in which Russell made his first entrance from a coffin propped against the back wall.

[195]

For many years these plays were performed to capacity audiences and tickets were like the proverbial gold-dust. But that wasn't enough for the workaholic Mr Hunter who also appeared at lunchtimes in a revue, written by Gordon and usually performed with a Scottish actress-singer. It was while watching one of these that the idea occurred to me of putting together a tough, abrasive little Glaswegian and a toffee-nosed, condescending, blazer-clad Englishman. They would share a language, just about, but precious little else. Gordon Smith liked the idea and agreed to write a script for us for the following year. His son, Sean, joined us on electric piano and together we performed this show, *Scots Wha Who?* with great success. Our venue was a night club over a roller-skating disco and had the name, of which Russell always reminded audiences with blood-curdling relish, of 'The Bermuda Triangle'. Over the two weeks our audiences grew until we were playing to more than the legal or comfortable capacity and even then turning customers away.

It was suggested to me that if I wanted to repeat the exercise the following year it would have to be for the full three weeks of the festival, for otherwise it meant Russell and Gordon losing six potentially lucrative performances. I readily agreed and arranged to stay on after 'Round Midnight's run had finished. Gordon wrote, I thought, an even better script but such is the fickle contrariness of the theatre-going public that we enjoyed far less success. The strain of two demanding performances every day, over a period of about twelve hours, was also beginning to tell on Russell and the following year he decided to do his revues at midnight, about half an hour after his play finished, which meant that, sadly, we were neither of us able to appear on the other's show. A few years later Russell suffered a heart attack, despite this change, and for the first time in my experience was unable to appear at all during the festival. Happily I hear that he recovered and I have little doubt is now overdoing it as usual.

Stella Hanson, whom I mentioned in connection with the programmes at Chichester, was obliged to leave 'Round Midnight' and indeed the BBC for a couple of years during which time she went to live in New York where her husband was temporarily employed. However, on her return she rejoined the Corporation and it was not long before she was appointed editor of my programme; it began to scale undreamed-of heights, gaining in the process a great reputation in the realms of theatre and publishing. Under her guidance we embarked on a schedule of outside broadcasts at least once a month, in addition to Edinburgh, Belfast and Chichester, and for two years running we broadcast live for a week by satellite link from New York.

Another of Stella's ploys in Edinburgh was to pack more and more into our shows from the Caledonian Hotel, gradually building up over the week so that on our last night we would feature as many as fifteen or sixteen attractions during the course of our two hours. This was an amazing technical achievement apart from anything else, since our stage was quite small and often it was necessary for successive groups to share piano and drums, while front-line microphones had to be moved and changed to accommodate different instruments and singers. As most of the acts were usually in transit either to or from their own shows our planned running order could never be more than an approximate guide and I had to be ready at perhaps a few seconds' notice to change the expected link and introduce a different act all together – at the same time keeping an eye on the studio manager effecting the microphone changes around me, for it was little use winding up an announcement before he was ready. That did happen sometimes, but rarely, thanks to the outstanding efficiency of Mark Farrar, a regular member of our team, and, in my opinion, irreplaceable. His days were longer than anyone's, with the exception of Stella, for he would accompany me all over the city to record location interviews as required, then attend sound checks in the afternoon, and follow that with the shows at night. And he still found time to visit shows to find acts to recommend to us.

Another hazard in presenting these broadcasts live lay in the way some artists, usually jazz musicians and lesser comics, would get quite carried away in performance and far exceed the eight or ten minutes allotted to them. This self indulgence never paid off because the audience inevitably grew restless, acts due to appear later suffered by having their time ration cut, and we seldom used the offenders again. By the same token, those who could be counted on to behave professionally would be re-booked year after year.

We were delighted, for instance, to find in a small cocktail bar one year the polished double act who call themselves 'Kit and the Widow' with their original, sophisticated and frequently risqué material. They became great favourites with our audiences and their own stage shows eventually attracted capacity crowds as well.

Another artist who became a regular and is now a household name was the brilliant impressionist Rory Brenner. I think his act is now far and away the best in that highly competitive field and one of the many things we liked best about him was that he was still prepared to join us in our rumbustious Calley shows after he had become a famous television name, which is sadly more than can be said for some.

The harmony group Cantabile became, as it were, friends of the family, too. They took part in 'Round Midnight' from many venues all over the country, and on one occasion even came up to Edinburgh to be with us on our last night even though they were not appearing elsewhere in the city. In 1988 we were both nominated for the Dankworth's International Allmusic Awards and no one could have been more warmly congratulatory than Cantabile when I won. I was more than happy to reciprocate the following year when they gained the award in their category.

John Drummond's successor as the artistic director of the Edinburgh Festival was the theatre director Frank Dunlop. An affable man, highly respected in his own particular sphere, I think he strengthened the theatre side of events but I fear his knowledge of music and musicians is inadequate for this demanding job. The finest artists in the world of opera, concert and recital almost invariably have to be booked two or three years in advance; the failure to understand this inevitably leads to the use of the second division, who are available at shorter notice. At all events the Festivals of '88 and '89 seemed to me to have declined in stature; we certainly decided that there were insufficient attractions to justify two weeks of broadcasts and cut our stay down to five nights, with two studio programmes devoted to main festival events and only three shows from the Caledonian.

This decline, if such it is, has coincided with the expansion of the Glasgow Mayfest and I think, had 'Round Midnight' continued, we should by now be paying more attention to that event. Whether it will ever take over from Edinburgh as Europe's major arts festival is something of a moot point, but one man who has firmly placed a foot in both camps is Bill Burdett Coutts; some years ago he achieved a revolution on the Edinburgh Fringe by acquiring the capacious Assembly Rooms in George Street, adapting six or seven of them as theatres of varying size, and himself booking acts to fill each venue from morning till late night in place of the traditional fringe free-for-all. He has since started to put acts into Glasgow as well, but denies any knowledge of a take-over by that West Side city. I shall observe future developments with interest.

[24]

When the suggestion was made that 'Round Midnight' might visit New York to present five live shows linked to Britain by satellite, my opportunist friend Steve Allen was soon in on the act, keen to get us there. The BBC, as trustees of public funds, quite rightly despatches its minions to various parts of the world at tourist rates. If those minions can make their own arrangements to be upgraded without further expense, so be it. Steve, needless to say, knew the right people to approach and, in return for photographs and an article for British Airways' in-house magazine, we were transferred to first class.

During the outward flight a steward invited me to visit the flight deck – a great thrill, but an even greater one was in store. As we approached New York the captain sent back another message to the effect that there was a free crew seat available if I would care to join them for landing. We took our place in the spiral of traffic and I was amazed to see the quantity of aircraft in close proximity to each other. We had already started to descend when there was an apparently unexpected wind shift through ninety degrees and all the aircraft in view, as well as our own, started to climb again and reposition for landing at a different angle of approach. It was a rare privilege and a thrill to witness this aspect of a transatlantic journey.

I was strapped into my seat well away from any controls, of course, but nevertheless found myself reminded of a visit to the bridge of the *Canberra* on a Mediterranean cruise years earlier. This was also a working trip, recording programmes with Ray Davies and the Button Down Brass that included interviews and commentaries describing life aboard and our visits to Athens,

Naples and Majorca. During one passage a friendly officer, who knew of my interest in sailing, took me up on to the bridge and on this occasion I was invited, briefly, to take the wheel. In a short space of time we were well off course and the wheel was snatched from my hands with a muttered, 'Bloody 'ell, sir, you'll 'ave us over like a bloody destroyer.'

Our main purpose in visiting America with 'Round Midnight' was to give British listeners who might never have the opportunity of going there themselves some idea of life, and especially artistic life, in the Big Apple. We also set out to obtain interviews with famous names who in some cases would be unavailable elsewhere. This meant living and working at high pressure, of course, and packing more experience into a few days than one would normally expect to do in months; it's the sort of life-style on which I find I thrive and I would happily have stayed there for much longer. Indeed in that respect I envy Jonathan King, who has established for himself very firm footholds in both worlds and is able to work alternately in London and New York, with homes in both.

Our 'Round Midnight' team on the first trip consisted of Stella Hanson and myself, Steve Allen, two other producers and a production assistant, and Tom Boswell who is a sort of broadcasting jack of all trades, best known for programmes on motoring and rowing perhaps, but with us on this occasion to handle publicity and to operate recording equipment for me on our treks round town. Due to a misunderstanding over hotel bookings our little group was split up on arrival and I found myself in a smallish establishment somewhere in the Eighties, adjacent to the middle section of Central Park. It was unfashionable and relatively inexpensive but I liked it and soon found that I could walk nearly everywhere I had to, or wanted to, go. I seldom took cabs and never set foot on the subway. On our most active day Tom and I walked a distance of sixteen miles during the process of recording eight interviews; he calculated this after the event.

Our base of operations was the BBC's own suite of studios in the Rockefeller Center, between Fifth and Sixth Avenues, mainly used for news reports and also where Alastair Cooke records his 'Letter from America'. They were not used to music programmes but were able to lash up sufficient equipment in the way of record players and tape machines to meet our requirements. Of course, due to the time difference between New York and London, I was going on air there between six and eight p.m., and the programmes were being heard in Britain at their normal time of eleven p.m. to one a.m. Some guests agreed to come to be interviewed in the studio, but in most cases Tom and I went to them in their homes or offices. Dame Kiri Te Kanawa was also on a brief visit to promote some of her records, but I missed her on a personal appearance at one of New York's biggest record stores and had to settle for recording a telephone conversation.

Someone I was looking forward to meeting again, having first interviewed him in London, was Arthur Mitchell, the first black dancer to have been a principal with New York City Ballet. He had studied with Balanchine, and was himself the founder of the Dance Theater of Harlem. He came to the studio in Rockefeller Centre but also invited me on my last morning to visit him at the school in Harlem where I might sit in on his class. This for once was way beyond walking distance and as my cab drove further and further north I began to worry about the return journey. The buildings became more and more forbidding, many of them in an advanced state of disrepair or else boarded up and unoccupied, and I became aware that cabs were very few and far between. I asked my driver if I should have much trouble finding one and he said that I sure would, but maybe the school would be able to help.

Whatever the difficulties and my misgivings, the visit was far more than just worthwhile. Although many people interested in dance are admirers of Arthur Mitchell's work I think few can be aware of the full extent and importance of what he has achieved in Harlem. His school is situated in an area where drugs are an enormous problem among young people, but in addition to training future professionals Arthur has lured many youngsters off the street and into his classrooms as a healthier and more interesting way of utilising their leisure time. He is rightly and deeply adored by countless thousands in the community.

Shortly before my visit Arthur Mitchell had had two accidents which had injured his back. He was in pain and under treatment but still took class himself, apologising for not being able to demonstrate what he was talking about and asking one of the senior students to do it for him. As time went on, his enthusiasm took over and he started to do quite difficult movements until a particularly strenuous kick made him stop and, placing one hand on his spine, he said, 'Oh, I think I just put my back "in"!'

I was fascinated to watch this master at work, and even more to see how the students under his direction improved quite perceptibly in a very short space of time. We also had a fruitful discussion, during which we set up a feature to be recorded at the Dance Theater of Harlem's next visit to the Coliseum in London.

The secretary did indeed call a cab for me and as I stood outside waiting for it to arrive I was charmed by the number of young people who came to me and thanked me for visiting their school.

I long ago came to the conclusion that in the arts, and entertainment generally, it is always the nicest and most talented people who behave as though you were doing them a favour by talking to them and always the second-raters who put on airs and graces quite inappropriate to their importance or ability.

Someone else who reinforced that opinion on this first week of programmes from New York was the opera singer Robert Merrill. His is a voice I had known and admired for as long as I could remember, yet here was this great star of the Met, specially chosen by Toscanini to sing the baritone roles in broadcast performances of *La Traviata* and *Un Ballo in Maschera*, an artist who had sung to great acclaim in Milan, Venice and Paris, chatting away to me in an accent that became broader and broader Brooklynese by the minute.

One of the shows I went to see on Broadway was the musical adaptation of Dickens' *Mystery of Edwin Drood* with Cleo Laine scoring a great success in the role of Mrs Puffer. The story itself was

[203]

set in an old time music hall which, being something of a novelty to American audiences, was drawing the town. When it eventually came to London at the Savoy it had nothing like the same appeal and I think Cleo was wise to opt not to do it. However, she had been playing in New York for about a year when I saw it; she lived in a flat she and John Dankworth had had there for some time, by chance quite close to the hotel in which I was staying. Cleo told me this had once been a notorious drugs district, known locally as Needle Alley, but had recently cleaned up its image and now housed many attractive and fashionable small restaurants. I think she was glad to see someone from home after such a long time, and after we had recorded a longish interview in the flat she insisted on taking Tom Boswell and me to a splendid lunch.

Another expatriate, though in his case on a much more permanent basis, who also received us most warmly was the British actor Jim Dale. He has lived in New York for something like ten years now and his home is high in a skyscraper on Sixth Avenue. He had a balcony garden way up there, with trees and shrubs incongruously growing on the side of this highrise building, and there we were able to record an interview without interference from the bustling traffic below. Jim was not working on that occasion, but when I went back a year later he was the popular star of the Broadway production of *Me and My Girl* and had just signed a contract for an extended run in that musical. I went to see the production and was amazed by the anglicisation of the American actors around him and, to a lesser extent, by the near-hysterical enthusiasm of the members of the American public around me.

A composer of hit shows who agreed to appear on my programme was Jerry Herman, who had written *The Pajama Game*, *Damn Yankees* and the work which, despite several false alarms, has still not been given a West End production, *Mack and Mabel*. Jerry is one of the few people in New York who lives in a house as opposed to an apartment and it comes as something of a surprise in that concrete jungle to look out of a sitting room window and see a rear garden with grass and trees. And that followed the first surprise: a welcome at the front door from a rather camp, white-coated black butler. This dignitary ushered us up to the first floor where Jerry was working at his grand piano; he broke off immediately to give us all the time we needed. At that time he was seriously hoping that *Mack and Mabel* was going into the West End and that he would be there to see it. His greatest problem is that he has an illness that completely rules out flying so he has to make even the longest journeys by sea. Unfortunately that production turned out to be yet another non-starter.

It was also an extraordinary experience to meet the famous band-leader Woody Herman, whose records I had bought and enjoyed since boyhood. He was by this time, I believe, seventy-eight years old, but was still touring with his band and playing as many as two hundred engagements a year. There was something sad about this frail old man, forced to undertake such a heavy work load mainly to pay back taxes. He still trotted out the cynical one-liner jokes that are so often the stock in trade of jazz musicians, but there was no joy in them. We recorded the interview in a fairly small and rather plain hotel room and, strangely, the abiding picture I have in my mind is of a tiny, untouched dish of strawberries on his dressing table.

Woody had died by the time of my second visit to New York when I met an even older member of the jazz fraternity, Max Gordon, the owner of the jazz club The Village Vanguard in the far from salubrious basement of a bar in Greenwich Village. Max was in his nineties but still visited the club every day and was happy to reminisce about some of the famous names who had started their careers under his roof. He too is no longer with us and his name joins the list of those I am thankful I met just in time.

On the second and as it turned out the last time that 'Round Midnight' went to New York I invited my son Christopher to join me for a few days, a prospect which excited him very much. He actually arrived on the evening that I went to The Village Vanguard and I remember he sat at a pavement table outside the club staring at the streams of yellow cabs which he had only ever seen, of course, on movies and television. Like the steam which pours out of the gratings in the middle of the road, yellow cabs are just another of the commonplace sights that somehow shout 'New York'.

On this visit the production team had asked me if there was anybody I should ideally like to interview if they could fix it; without stopping to think I said, 'Katherine Hepburn,' without believing for a moment there would be any chance of meeting her. By happy coincidence a book had just been published in the States by Miss Hepburn about the making of *The African Queen* and it seemed she was happy to give an interview if we promised to hold it until publication in Britain. So, Christopher, Tom Boswell and I duly found ourselves on the pavement outside a small brownstone house, rather ahead of schedule and very excited. Tom whizzed round the corner to a florist's to buy some roses and during his absence a lady whom we rightly took to be a housekeeper came down the street, looked rather askance at Chris and me and disappeared into the basement. Then, on the dot of eleven o'clock, the time of our appointment, the front door flew open and there was Katherine Hepburn herself, in sweater, slacks and running shoes. Before we had time to get over our surprise, that familiar voice, with drawl and quaver just as we had heard them so many times, said, 'C'mon in, fellers.'

Although practically eighty years old this screen goddess was still extremely beautiful. She had, sadly, developed an illness which caused a shaking of the head and trembling of the hands but they were almost completely disguised by her wit and personality. At first a little disconcerted because she thought we were from television and she hadn't had her hair done, when it transpired we were radio people she relaxed and talked freely about anything we chose – including her relationship with Spencer Tracy which had always been taboo during Tracy's own lifetime.

I had once been given an explanation by an English actor of why Tracy always seemed to make his first entrance in movies with a long walk into close-up, looking down until the last second, when he glanced straight into camera. He was looking for his mark on the studio floor, I was told. It seemed plausible at the time. I asked if there was anything in this story and Miss Hepburn first looked dumbfounded then roared with laughter saying, 'What nonsense. He was a professional, he knew where his mark was.'

At the end of our conversation Katherine asked me, with genuine modesty, whether I thought people today would be interested in what she had to say. I told her that for the previous twenty-four hours I had been telling everybody I met that I was going to meet her, from bellhops to barmen, from taxi-drivers to waiters, and without exception they had expressed their envy of my good fortune. 'Everybody loves you,' I assured her. She pondered this for a moment, and then uttered the unforgettable line: 'It just goes to show, if you live long enough you get over-appreciated.'

I haven't seen too many signs of that happening to me yet, so I think there must be rather more to it, somehow. I have learned one thing about the advancing years, however, and that is one seldom realises, when relishing an experience, that it might be for the last time. New York was a good example, for while working flat out trying to make as much use as possible of every minute I'm sure at the back of my mind I was noting some things I hoped to cover on the next trip. Like Off Broadway and even 'Off Off Broadway', for example. And how I longed to see the Free Theater presented in Central Park by Joe Papp, with major actors in classic plays. Unfortunately I just missed *Twelfth Night* with Murray Abrahams, who was so impressive as Salieri in the film version of *Amadeus*, playing Malvolio.

Unfortunately it was not deemed justifiable to send 'Round Midnight' to America the following year, and by the spring of 1990 there was no 'Round Midnight' to send anywhere.

[25]

'Round Midnight' was my own personal longest running radio show, and so many episodes deserve a mention.

We always had a close working relationship with the National Theatre; many leading actors and directors have come straight from there in the middle of the night to be interviewed. Whenever possible I tried to see a performance, either a preview or a matinee, before talking to the people concerned with a play, and I think this helped to establish a closer rapport with members of the profession than might otherwise have been the case.

Two of our most exciting outside broadcasts were transmitted from the foyer of the National and, needless to say, they were star studded, for we had the casts from three theatres to draw on and many of those who were not going to take part in the broadcasts stayed along with members of the public as a large and enthusiastic audience. On one occasion the veteran actress Ellen Pollock was celebrating her birthday; during the first part of our show Alec McCowen took her for supper in the restaurant at a table looking down on the area in which we were performing. When she was happily wined and dined he brought her down without warning her; she instantly became the hit of the show, delivering wonderful and just slightly outrageous anecdotes in true grande dame manner.

That was a night on which we also went perhaps a little OTT and featured a juggler. I did a commentary on his act and we included the audience reaction. The climax of his performance was sensational. He juggled with a piece of French bread to which he had set fire, an egg and a frying pan, then suddenly stopped keeping them in the air, caught the egg in the pan thereby cracking it and finally fried it by holding the burning bread underneath.

Among the musical acts were the singing group Cantabile, who were appearing in the musical show *Blondel* further down the road at the Old Vic. They were playing the part of monks and, as there was not time to change between their performance and mine, they ran along the Waterloo Road in their brown habits, which must have been a sight worth seeing.

I must just add that, like John Drummond in Edinburgh, Sir Peter Hall at the National Theatre always went out of his way to make a very positive contribution to our programmes. I think he recognised that we were helping to carry out something which was always part of his policy for the South Bank building – to make it a really lively venue where something entertaining was going on for as many hours of the day and night as possible.

There are memories to be treasured, too, of a show we put on in the far more intimate surroundings of the little Stephen Joseph Theatre in Scarborough where Alan Ayckbourn first produces his plays as well as putting on many others that are never seen anywhere else. The year we went there was also the one that marked the end of Max Jaffa's reign as the king of light music; he gave daily performances at the Floral Hall where he had been in residence every summer for twenty-five years. Obviously we had to feature Max on the show with his singer wife Jean; the rest of the music was supplied by a talented folk trio from the North East and the flamenco guitarist Juan Martin.

Now the Stephen Joseph Theatre is, as I said, quite small, and tends to attract a fairly mature audience. How we were likely to fare was a moot point. To our immense delight, the auditorium was full and stayed that way until we had finished. Alan Ayckbourn himself made a lengthy and entertaining appearance and all in all we had another hit on our hands.

The last departure from the normal 'Round Midnight' routine occurred in the summer of 1988 when we took the show on a tour of seaside resorts for a week. In order to make this workable, Stella Hanson decided to add a couple of solo musicians to the regular

[209]

team; they could be relied on to do as much or as little as required with a minimum amount of sound check rehearsal and without giving the balance engineers undue problems. These two were Juan Martin, who had been in the Scarborough show, and the pianist Brooks Aaron, often heard these days presenting his own programme with the BBC Concert Orchestra.

Our first show was, inevitably, Blackpool, where we played a couple of nights; that town remains the holiday showbiz centre of Britain for the summer season, with far and away the greatest number of acts appearing there simultaneously. The venue in which we performed was a very bizarre hall called the Spanish Room within the Winter Garden complex. It could seat several hundred and the decoration which gave rise to the name consisted of three-dimensional models of Spanish villages, with lights in all the windows, built into each of the four corners.

The musical acts we added for the two nights there were Humphrey Lyttleton and his band, playing if anything better than in all the years I had known them, and the rumbustious cockney group fronted by Chas and Dave, who were noisy but great fun.

The weather for this part of the tour was predictably appalling and there are few more depressing sights than Blackpool front in pouring, blinding rain. As I descended the hotel staircase to breakfast after our first show a lady polishing the brass strips of the steps looked up and said in a broad Lancashire voice, 'Mornin'.' I responded that in my view it wasn't very good, to which she added, 'Ah didn't say it were good. Ah just said "mornin'".'

Blackpool always seems to have provided me with experiences to be remembered, like the drunken escapade with Clinton Ford recounted elsewhere in this story. This time the performance highlight came when I attempted to play straight man to the wonderful Les Dawson; and the after hours moment, back at the hotel, when Juan Martin and Chas struck up an unlikely friendship, with Juan showing Chas the rudiments of flamenco guitar and Chas returning the compliment by showing Juan rock and roll chords.

After Blackpool we were scheduled to play the following night in

Paignton; the only practical way of making the journey was to drive, so we hired a couple of cars and divided into two teams. One consisted of the production staff and the other of myself, Graham Lambourn, our publicity man on this tour, and Juan and Brooks Aaron. Graham and I shared the driving, to the silent terror of the two musicians; I had agreed to appear for an interview on Radio Devon in Exeter at three in the afternoon, so we went like bats out of hell. On the way we stopped off at a country pub for lunch and, as the four of us filed through the bar to the rear garden, with Juan carrying his precious guitar, a maiden seated on a bar stool asked 'Eh, are you a band?' I think our musicians were slightly insulted but Graham and I were quite flattered.

We arrived in Paignton at almost the same time as Her Majesty the Queen, but I think this was purely by chance! The Royal Yacht *Britannia* was anchored in the bay and the town was full to bursting, but not many came to our show that night. I think this was due as much to the lack of space in the foyer of the theatre as anything, because those who did attend enjoyed a bill that included Cannon and Ball, Bernie Winters and colleagues from nearby Babbacombe, Helen Shapiro, and once again our wonderful Cantabile.

From Paignton it was on once more, through thick fog this time, to Bournemouth for a show in the relatively new BIC. This is a large multi-purpose venue which was ideally suited to our needs, with an enormous foyer where four hundred people eventually sat and watched 'Round Midnight'. They were delighted by the stylish if now rather rotund George Melly and also had the questionable pleasure of watching me interview Michael Barrymore while he stood on his head. He said he didn't think the radio audience would appreciate this but I assured him that he sounded quite different that way up.

The tour was generally considered by all to be a success and the thought was certainly in mind to repeat the exercise the following year. Unfortunately, when we started to look into possibilities we found that all the same artists were on hand, so it was decided to drop the project.

[211]

Then something of a bombshell was delivered; Stella Hanson was taken off the programme and transferred initially to the John Dunn show. I suppose I should have at that stage read the writing on the wall, for it seemed to be the intention of the management from then on to run the programme down. Stella's replacement had admittedly asked for the editorial job but soon found it was not really his territory and the show undoubtedly began to suffer, not least from a lack of outside broadcasts. He was eventually moved elsewhere and my final editor was Richard Masters, who had for a while been number two to Stella. He soon set about restoring much that had been lost and was able to ensure that when we were eventually axed at the end of March 1990 we were able to go out in style with the *Showboat* outside broadcast from Stratford on Avon that I've already written about.

Something that all Radio Two programmes take part in each year is the great Children in Need campaign. In my final full year I thought I should like to try to make a personal contribution and offered to do a one man show at lunchtime wherever we were on the road. It was an adaptation of a four voice anthology of verse and speeches from plays on the overall theme of the Seven Ages of Man from Shakespeare's *As You Like It* that we had done some time before in our own little theatre at home. I wish I could say that it was a resounding success, but alas it wasn't. Attendances were small, but at least patrons were generous so that I was able in the end to make a reasonable donation. The first performance was at the Watermill Theatre in Hungerford, then I gave another in the new Minerva Theatre at Chichester, and Pamela joined me in turning it into a two-hander for a week at The Pleasance during the Edinburgh Festival. The interesting suggestion was made there that we should have done better to charge admission rather than, as we did, perform free with a collection at the end. Then finally I resorted to the solo format for a performance in Belfast.

By this time I knew that 'Round Midnight' was to be dropped from the schedules and so, as I headed into my own sixth and seventh ages, I had to decide what to try to do with the rest of my life. One kind listener wrote to suggest I had had a good run and asked why I didn't accept the inevitable and retire gracefully to enjoy whatever was left. I'm afraid that didn't and still doesn't appeal to me, so it was decision time, resulting in what will be the last chapter of the story.

[26]

To tell the truth there was a period during 1989 when I might have left full time employment by the BBC of my own volition before the decision was taken out of my hands. Pamela and I had been discussing a possible change for some time because we felt the need for some kind of stimulus as we headed for the last few laps.

I had known for some time that John Gale was leaving the Chichester Festival Theatre after five years as artistic director and the post was soon to be advertised. It seemed a long shot but I decided, along with many others far more qualified for the job than I, to submit an application. I could not claim long experience in a similar role elsewhere, but felt that many years' devotion to theatre generally, with a wide connection among actors, directors and writers, might just lend an aura of suitability. It was, nevertheless, quite a surprise to be invited to lunch by the chairman of the board of governors, Kenneth Fleet, to discuss my ideas. However, the decision went against me and as it happens a terrible mistake was made in the appointment. The man offered the job started to direct a play during the end of John Gale's reign so that there would sensibly be a period of overlap, then quite unaccountably decided that he didn't want the post after all and quite literally walked out, unforgivably abandoning a cast half-way through a production. Needless to say I hastily sent in a further application but by this time the job had gone to Michael Rudman who had worked for many years at the National. On the strength of his first season it is proving a sound appointment.

Michael is a Texan who came to Britain thirty years ago and stayed. He studied at Oxford, where he became President of the

Oxford University Dramatic Society, and in the ensuing years has run several theatres as well as working in the West End. He has an inexhaustible capacity for work, spending very few hours away from the theatre. He truly cares about the actors with whom he works, which is a great deal more than can be said about many other directors with unbelievably inflated egos, and he also seems to me to have great flair for selling his ideas to both the public and the press.

So Pamela and I decided as our next move to attempt to get back into theatre as actors. I was encouraged to take this step by the realisation that there are many roles, especially in the classics, for older players. Admittedly more for men than for women. Furthermore, while the profession is undeniably overcrowded with young aspirants, it seems that at the other end of the age range they are a good deal thinner on the ground. This opinion was recently endorsed by the director of the Royal Lyceum in Edinburgh who told me that even those who had stayed the course were in many cases reluctant to travel far from London where they preferred to sit waiting for television parts or lucrative commercial voice-overs.

Our next step was to write to Michael Rudman at Chichester and ask whether he would be interested in a couple of wrinklies who could still stand up and utter lines. He replied almost by return and asked me to ring him. He said that although he knew my work in radio he had of course no idea of any potential I might have as an actor. Would I, he wondered, be prepared to do an audition? When I agreed to this he arranged to see both of us in a couple of days' time in London when he would be at the Drury Lane Theatre.

This was fairly short notice, but fortunately we both had one-person performances up our sleeves from which we could find suitable speeches and we had in the past played the leads in our own production of *The Lion in Winter*, that fanciful tale about Henry II and his wife, Eleanor of Aquitaine. A hectic weekend of intensive rehearsal knocked a scene from that into some sort of shape.

We had both forgotten what it felt like to do auditions but soon discovered that nothing changes; you wake up on the day feeling sick and go through the whole procedure in a sort of daze.

[215]

When we arrived at Drury Lane, early, Michael came out of the audition room to greet us and said that the previous applicant was about to do his thing and was preparing himself for it. His rendition of Doctor Caius, the French physician in *Merry Wives of Windsor*, was soon echoing round the walls in a powerful voice that didn't do anything to make us feel better.

At last it was our turn, and Michael spent a time chatting to us in a very general sort of way and then asked us if we would like to read something for him. He seemed quite surprised when I said we would like to play a scene, but asked me to set it up with an explanation of what had happened up to the point at which we planned to start and of the relationship between the two characters.

We set a couple of chairs in position as rehearsed but couldn't have got off to a more disastrous start. The scene began with a line from Pamela, after which there was silence. I was staring at a chair beside me thinking how strange it looked and not at all like the one I had been regarding for hours at home in rehearsals. It then dawned on me that I ought to be speaking and had almost certainly blown the audition without uttering a syllable.

The only thing to do was to apologise and start again, after which it all went fairly smoothly and Michael kindly listened to the whole scene which was of some ten minutes' duration. To our delighted astonishment he then said, 'Well, I think we can definitely find something for you. Go home and read the play and tell me what you'd like to play. Only don't ask for the lead.'

'He could do it very well,' said Pamela with commendable wifely loyalty. 'I'm sure he could,' continued Michael, 'but I've already cast it, and anyway I think you should ease yourself back in without the added burden of carrying the play.' He then went on to itemise the several good supporting roles that were still available, but said there was nothing left for Pamela. She immediately offered to understudy both the Merry Wives and got the job. I asked for the part of Shallow and got that, so there we were, back in the fold. There was just one little snag. Rehearsals were scheduled to start during the last week in March and I was contracted to 'Round Midnight' until the end of the month.

'That's OK,' said Michael. 'You can commute.' And incredible though it now seems that's exactly what I did. Richard Masters fixed up extra interviews to record in the weeks prior to my departure and BBC management kindly agreed to lay on a car to drive me back to Chichester every night after the broadcast.

Before all that, however, there was the matter of accommodation to organise. Chichester isn't really commutable for many actors and most are obliged to stay in the area, to which end the theatre has a lady with a list of flats, rooms and cottages that can be rented. We decided, though, that we could live happily on our boat which we had fortuitously moved from the Hamble river to Chichester Yacht Basin the previous year. It's quite roomy for two people and a small dog and with mains electricity available alongside we were able to instal a heater and a portable television, making it a home from home and just ten minutes' drive away from work. Mind you, the end of March is a little early for boat dwelling even on the south coast, and for the first couple of weeks we often awoke to find ice inside the windows.

The great thing about the overlap of jobs, albeit for only a week, was that there was no trauma of suddenly being out of work and facing unwanted early retirement. I still had my Transcription radio programme 'Top of the Pops' to do and from the Saturday morning following the very last 'Round Midnight' I also took over Radio Two's popular 'Sounds of the Sixties'. As I write they both continue.

It must be admitted for all that, the last week of 'Round Midnight', and especially the very last night of all, were physically, mentally and emotionally draining. I had been inundated with letters lamenting the demise of the show and it really did feel like suddenly being cut off from a whole host of friends. Colleagues at the BBC were immensely supportive and many of them either dropped in or phoned to say goodbye. Two studio managers with whom I had often worked, Mike Robinson and Edward de Bono, generously sent in a magnum of champagne. I tried to maintain control right to the end but have to confess with very little shame that in the final moment I was in floods of tears.

Once again, as when playing in pantomime many years previously, I had certain misgivings about how fellow actors might react to my presence. They nearly all seemed to have worked with each other in the past and although many of them had been interviewed by me over the years would they, I couldn't help wondering, regard me as some sort of intruder? I needn't have worried, for it would be impossible to find a more friendly group of people both on stage and back stage.

Playing the leading role of Falstaff was the bluff, forthright and tremendously conscientious Bill Maynard. When I had first met him he was a very popular stand-up comedian but in the intervening years had established a deserved reputation on stage and television as a serious actor. Of substantial build in the first place, he had added another couple of stone to his bulk in preparation for the most famous fat man in literature. With his bald pate and a luxuriant beard, specially grown, he looked the part to perfection. He had worked with Michael Rudman at Nottingham Playhouse more than twenty years previously and often enjoyed remarking that the return engagement had been a long time coming.

Less than a year before coming to Chichester Bill had married the Belgian cabaret artiste Tonia Bern, the widow of Donald Campbell, but she preferred to live in Los Angeles and we only saw her on a brief visit. I think Bill was rather lonely, for he always welcomed company after the show, either in the pub or back for a take-away Chinese supper to the delightful little house he had rented. He was always extremely friendly towards Pamela and myself, and we shall remember that brief period of working with him with real affection.

Being an understudy is a fairly unrewarding job. Pamela used to say she felt like the spectre at the feast, for no matter how much she might admire Penelope Keith and Phyllida Law who played

[218]

Mistress Ford and Mistress Page respectively there was always in her mind a burning desire to go on and play one of the roles herself. She also added that in the highly unlikely event of both ladies being indisposed simultaneously her ingenuity would be stretched to the limit. It must be recorded that both actresses could not have been nicer and Phyllida even went through the lines with Pamela, which was just as well since surprisingly there was never a single understudy rehearsal. Come to think of it, with one other minor exception there were no understudies!

Penny Keith was one of the few company members able to commute, but even so it meant a nightly drive of some forty miles after the show. She was very amused on one occasion to overhear a member of the public say, 'Of course, it's an ideal place for her to be. She only lives down the road.' Husband Roddy, the former police detective Penelope had met on a previous stint in Chichester, was often in attendance and so, once or twice, were the two delightful sons they have adopted.

Michael Rudman had certainly assembled a talented and experienced company for his first Chichester production and one felt honoured to be a member of it. Richard Moore, who played Master Ford, Peter Bourke (Doctor Caius), Antony Brown (Sir Hugh Evans), and Graham Sinclair (Slender) had all had spells at the Royal Shakespeare Company, while Peter, Antony and Graham, together with Phyllida Law, Barbara Ferris (Mistress Quickly) and others had all been at the National.

At an early stage of rehearsal Michael surprised me by telling me that I was playing Shallow too old. When I protested that I had to say the line, 'I have lived four score year and upwards,' he said with never a pause, 'Change it. Make it three score.' Although nonplussed, I saw no point in starting off with a reputation for being difficult so I did my best to comply and in the event it did neither myself nor the play any harm.

As I have mentioned elsewhere, the structure of a season at Chichester is such that as soon as the first production is in performance the second one goes into rehearsal and thereafter there are always two in repertoire at any time. Michael had hoped to establish a considerable amount of through casting, thereby establishing a substantial company for the season, but he was not prepared to dictate casting to other directors. I had been sent scripts for the second play, *The Power and the Glory*, and the third, a Victorian melodrama called *The Silver King*, directed in turn by Tim Luscombe and Peter Wood, but although I was asked to read for the first of these unfortunately neither director considered me suitable for a part. This was a great disappointment as I loved being at Chichester and should have liked very much to stay for most of the season. On the other hand, had I done so I should have missed an opportunity of a once-in-a-lifetime broadcast which we shall come to shortly.

I was also to learn that getting a role doesn't necessarily mean keeping it. A very old friend of mine was eventually cast for the part in *Silver King* that I rather fancied myself and I feel bound to say that I thought he was an ideal choice. Unfortunately Peter Wood decided with less than two weeks to go to opening that he was unsuitable and cancelled the engagement, which must have been a shattering experience for him. Fairly nerve-racking, too, for Richard Moore, who took over at such short notice, but he acquitted himself marvellously.

The acting life is a vicious switch-back of promises, peaks, then fairly rapid dives down the other side into unemployment and despair. One hears this on many occasions, but I think most of us continue to harbour the quite irrational hope that we shall be the exception that proves the rule. At the beginning of the season there was at least a possibility that Pamela and I might be in two or three of the plays and there was even a suggestion that at the end *Merry Wives* could go on tour to Australia and California. After a bit this became just California and indeed discussions did continue for some time, only to fizzle out unsatisfactorily in the end. So, from a point at which employment for much of the year seemed to be on, as we neared the end of June unemployment reared its ugly head once more.

[220]

Then out of the blue came an enquiry from the BBC. Would I be interested in going to Rome to announce an open air concert on the eve of the World Cup Final with the three tenors Luciano Pavarotti, Placido Domingo and Jose Carreras, and two orchestras conducted by Zubin Mehta? Well, the day I say 'no' to a proposition like that is the day that pigs get wings. So, within days of leaving Chichester, Pamela and I were on a plane for the Italian capital and the most exciting concert we had either of us been to in our lives.

The setting for the performance was the ruins of the baths of the Emperor Caracalla which almost, but not quite I hope, defy description. Almost two thousand years old, there is enough left of the vast building to give a good idea of how awe-inspiring the original must have been. Two huge towers point to the sky and between them a vast stage has been constructed where opera and ballet performances are sometimes given. Arguably the three most famous tenors in the world today had agreed to appear for the first and almost certainly the last time together; each was to donate his fee to a charity of his choice. The programme was to consist of their own choice of favourite arias and popular songs. Inevitably there was a suggestion of contest about the event since to a large extent they share the same repertoire and Pavarotti and Domingo especially have often been presented in the press as great rivals. If you add to that the dramatic aspect that only two years earlier Carreras was desperately ill with leukaemia and had miraculously recovered you have all the ingredients for world-wide appeal. The concert was televised live to just about every country, recorded for release on disc, cassette and video, and Radio Two managed to get the British radio exclusive with, hopefully, several repeats possible in years to come.

On the night of my arrival in Rome there was a rehearsal on stage for orchestra and singers and I must say I fully expected the stars to mark their performances mainly for the benefit of the television cameras, but not these boys. Whether it was a combination of occasion, setting and songs, or whether it was more that they were shoulder to shoulder on the same stage I don't know, but they gave out with voice and emotion in the most thrilling style. Now all three singers have made recordings of 'Nessum Dorma' from *Turandot* which had been adopted as the World Cup theme song and it was Pavarotti who was to sing it at the concert, but it was interesting to note in rehearsal that the other two joined in like backing singers in the chorus section.

The next morning there was a press conference at a hotel in Rome which gave me my first close quarters experience of the famous paparazzi in action. In the centre of the hall, facing the artists, an enormous phalanx of photographers was jammed in as tightly as possible, firing away with their cameras as though these gentlemen had decreed that they would never ever be photographed again.

The introductions, most of the questions and all of the answers were spoken in Italian which made life a little difficult for some of us, but when an English woman journalist asked a question of Pavarotti it was enough to make us cringe with embarrassment. Was he upset, she asked, that Italy was no longer in the Cup? His normally benevolent smile froze on his lips, his eyes gave her the only answer she deserved, then he said with a politeness she didn't merit, 'My 'eart is still bleeding.'

The event itself more than fulfilled its promise. My only anxiety had been that there might be long delays between items as one singer made way for the next, so I had boned up on every bit of information I could get in order to be able to keep talking if necessary. To my astonishment they sped on and off like lightning. The concert ended with all three joining forces in a twenty minute medley: from time to time they sang duets and trios in which the blend of voices was nothing short of spine tingling. The packed audience, some of whom had paid as much as a thousand pounds for their tickets to touts on the actual day of the show, rose to their feet and cheered. The three singers returned and for their encore sang the whole medley again, followed that with all three of them singing 'Nessum Dorma' once more, and followed that with 'O Sole Mio'.

As a footnote to this story, one more surprise. At the end of the proceedings the Italian crowd of several thousands left the arena in almost complete silence, to stand quietly in line for buses and taxis with scarcely a murmur, giving no indication that they had just attended a concert the like of which would most probably never be heard again.

On returning to London I continued to work on this book, which I had started in Chichester, and again began the search for work on the stage. A couple of provincial theatres made initially encouraging noises which eventually led to nothing and then there was another exciting radio event. I had once suggested to the controller of Radio Two attempting to revive a broadcast of 'Saturday Club' in exactly the way we used to do it, with very few records and performances by groups and artists in our studio. She liked the idea, and sure enough when Ann Robinson moved over to deputise for Derek Jameson for a while I was asked to do two editions of the old show. We managed to gather artists who had all appeared on it several times in its heyday, Acker Bilk, Kenny Ball, Joe Brown, Marty Wilde, Susan Maughan, Danny Williams, Helen Shapiro, The Swinging Blue Jeans and The Tremeloes, and they all came up with cracking performances of their sixties hits. Listeners joined in the fun by sending in requests for their favourites of the period, and there we were on air in our original time slot from ten until twelve for a couple of Saturday mornings.

Although I was busy I still began to feel dispirited about my lack of success in reactivating a long-dormant theatrical career. I should know better and realise these things take time, but as even my best friends will tell you, I'm a born worrier.

Then lo and behold , as I drew near to the final paragraphs of this book I was asked to read for a leading part in a fringe production in London of *Lynchville* by Snoo Wilson; I got the job. By the time this is in print of course that will be history, or worse still already forgotten. But for now the adrenalin is pumping again, this is where I came in, and unless the manager decides to chuck me out, I really do intend to see the whole programme round again.

[223]